How to use your Snap Revision Workbook

This Reading Snap Workbook will help you to get a top mark in your AQA English Language exam. Questions and activities are divided into clear sections to work through and fully prepare for the exam.

Revise 1, 2 and 3
Short tasks progressing in level as you work through the topic.

Extend
More challenging activities to prepare you for the exam practice questions later in the book.

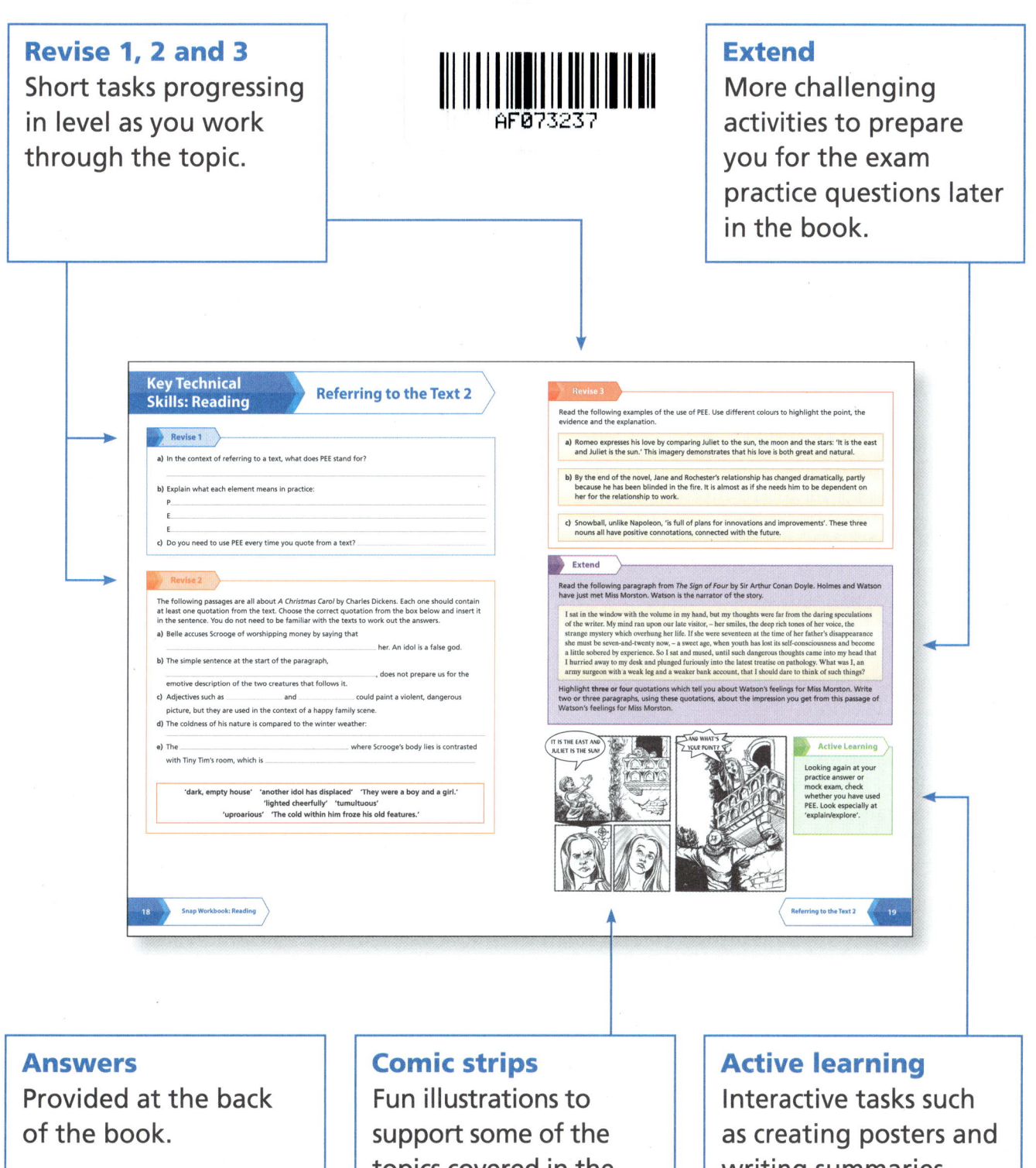

Answers
Provided at the back of the book.

Comic strips
Fun illustrations to support some of the topics covered in the book.

Active learning
Interactive tasks such as creating posters and writing summaries.

AUTHOR: PAUL BURNS

Published by Collins
An imprint of HarperCollins*Publishers*
1 London Bridge Street
London SE1 9GF

HarperCollins*Publishers*
Macken House
39/40 Mayor Street Upper
Dublin 1
D01 C9W8
Ireland

© HarperCollins*Publishers* Limited 2025

ISBN 9780008784607

First published 2025

10 9 8 7 6 5 4 3 2 1

All rights reserved. No part of this publication may be reproduced, stored in a retrieval system, or transmitted, in any form or by any means, electronic, mechanical, photocopying, recording or otherwise, without the prior permission of Collins.

Without limiting the exclusive rights of any author, contributor or the publisher of this publication, any unauthorised use of this publication to train generative artificial intelligence (AI) technologies is expressly prohibited. HarperCollins also exercise their rights under Article 4(3) of the Digital Single Market Directive 2019/790 and expressly reserve this publication from the text and data mining exception.

British Library Cataloguing in Publication Data.

A CIP record of this book is available from the British Library.

Author: Paul Burns
Contributor: Steve Eddy
Commissioning editor: Clare Souza
Project management: Shelley Teasdale and Richard Toms
Editorial: Fiona Watson
Typesetting: Jouve India Private Limited
Cover designers: Kneath Associates and Sarah Duxbury
Inside concept design: Ian Wrigley
Illustrations: Rose and Thorn Creative Services Ltd
Production: Bethany Brohm
Printed in the UK by Martins the Printer Ltd.

ACKNOWLEDGEMENTS
The author and publisher are grateful to the copyright holders for permission to use quoted materials and images.

Every effort has been made to trace copyright holders and obtain their permission for the use of copyright material. The author and publisher will gladly receive information enabling them to rectify any error or omission in subsequent editions. All facts are correct at time of going to press.

This book contains FSC™ certified paper and other controlled sources to ensure responsible forest management.

For more information visit: www.harpercollins.co.uk/green

Contents

Key Technical Skills: Reading
- Explicit Information and Ideas 1 4
- Explicit Information and Ideas 2 6
- Implicit Information and Ideas 1 8
- Implicit Information and Ideas 2 10
- Synthesis and Summary 1 12
- Synthesis and Summary 2 14
- Referring to the Text 1 16
- Referring to the Text 2 18
- Analysing Language 1 20
- Analysing Language 2 22
- Analysing Language 3 24
- Analysing Language 4 26
- Analysing Form and Structure 1 28
- Analysing Form and Structure 2 30

English Language
- Creative Reading 1 32
- Creative Reading 2 34
- Creative Reading 3 36
- Creative Reading 4 38
- Reading Non-fiction 1 40
- Reading Non-fiction 2 42
- Reading Non-fiction 3 44
- Reading Non-fiction 4 46

Exam Practice
- Paper 1, Reading 1 48
- Paper 1, Reading 2 51
- Paper 1, Reading 3 54
- Paper 1, Reading 4 57
- Paper 2, Reading 1 60
- Paper 2, Reading 2 64
- Paper 2, Reading 3 68
- Paper 2, Reading 4 72

Answers 76

Key Technical Skills: Reading

Explicit Information and Ideas 1

Revise 1

In the following passage, highlight words or phrases that tell you something about cheese.

> Cheeses are often associated with particular regions. People in the UK eat huge amounts of cheese every year. They also eat a lot of butter. Both cheese and butter are made from milk. Some people prefer other products to butter, both for health reasons and because they are easier to spread. Too much cheese might also be unhealthy.

Revise 2

Look at the following description.

> Mr Allworthy, who sold cheese in the market, was a large, ruddy-faced man of 53. He had been working there for over thirty years. There were quite a few other stallholders who were just as long-serving, among them Tricky Dicky, who sold electrical goods, Millie the fish woman, and the crockery seller, 'Smasher' Briggs. But Mr Allworthy was probably the most popular of them all. He was renowned for his friendly manner and his low prices. He was often helped out by his wife, a cheerful little woman who claimed she had never eaten cheese in her life and had no intention of starting now.

If you were asked to tick facts that the writer tells you about Mr Allworthy, which of the following answers would be correct?

a) Mr Allworthy sold cheese. ☐

b) Tricky Dicky sold electrical goods. ☐

c) Mr Allworthy was very popular. ☐

d) Mr Allworthy's prices were low. ☐

e) Mr Allworthy has six children. ☐

f) Mrs Allworthy never ate cheese. ☐

g) Mr Allworthy loved cheese. ☐

h) Mr Allworthy had worked at the market for over thirty years. ☐

> **Revise 3**

Look at Revise 2 again. Think about the answers that you haven't marked as correct. Explain why each one is not correct.

....
....
....
....

> **Extend**

Read the following passage from *The Strange Case of Dr Jekyll and Mr Hyde* by Robert Louis Stevenson.

> The solemn butler knew and welcomed him; he was subjected to no stage of delay, but ushered direct from the door to the dining room where Dr Lanyon sat alone over his wine. This was a hearty, healthy, dapper, red-faced gentleman, with a shock of hair prematurely white, and a boisterous and decided manner. At the sight of Mr Utterson, he sprang from his chair and welcomed him with both hands.

List **four** things that you learn about Dr Lanyon's appearance and character.

> **Active Learning**

Look around the room you are in now. Go into another room (taking paper and pen with you). When you get there, list **four** facts about the room you have just left.

Explicit Information and Ideas 1

Key Technical Skills: Reading

Explicit Information and Ideas 2

Revise 1

In the following passage, highlight words or phrases that tell you how the writer feels about school.

> Generally speaking, I would say I am a very happy sort of girl. But I don't like school. In fact, I hate it and I can't wait to leave. I'm always being accused of exaggerating (especially by Rhona, who loves school) or of being melodramatic (by my parents) but that is how I feel. I find the environment stifling. I find the lessons boring and irrelevant. I don't even like the depressing brutalist building. My only consolation is that I will be leaving at the end of the year.

Revise 2

Look at the following paragraph, reporting on a council meeting.

> The meeting opened with Dame Elizabeth Ponsonby thanking the retiring clerk for his many years of service. Dame Elizabeth then outlined the council's plans for the coming year, which she described as innovative and exciting. First, the town hall clock will be repaired (not the most exciting idea I've ever heard but I suppose it needs to be done). The council will make sure that the town is put 'firmly on the map' by increasing spending on publicity and tidying up the park (exciting?). Spending on care in the community will be maintained at current levels (innovative?) but to achieve this, one of the libraries will have to close (not really exciting or innovative). However, I am pleased to report that, as Lord Mayor, Dame Elizabeth will ensure that standards are maintained, as she plans to invest in a new official limousine.

If you were asked to tick the council's plans that are outlined in the passage, which of the following answers would be correct?

a) The plans are exciting and innovative. ☐

b) The town clock will be repaired. ☐

c) One of the libraries will close. ☐

d) There will be a new town clerk. ☐

e) Dame Elizabeth will give up the official limousine. ☐

f) The park will be tidied up. ☐

g) A new map of the town will be published. ☐

h) Spending on care in the community will be the same. ☐

Revise 3

Look at Revise 2 again. Think about the answers that you haven't marked as correct. Explain why each one isn't correct.

Extend

Read the following extract from *Father and Son*, the autobiography of the poet Edmund Gosse.

> Out of the darkness of my infancy there comes one flash of memory. I am seated alone, in my baby chair, at a dinner-table set for several people. Somebody brings in a leg of mutton, puts it down close to me, and goes out. I am again alone, gazing at two low windows, wide open upon a garden. Suddenly, noiselessly, a large, long animal (obviously a greyhound) appears at one window-sill, slips into the room, seizes the leg of mutton and slips out again. When this happened I could not yet talk. The accomplishment of speech came to me very late, doubtless because I never heard young voices. Many years later, when I mentioned this recollection, there was a shout of laughter and surprise: 'That, then, was what became of the mutton! It was not you, who, as your Uncle A. pretended, ate it up, in the twinkling of an eye, bone and all!'

Tick the **four** statements that are true.

a) Gosse has many memories from his infancy. ☐
b) Gosse remembers someone bringing a leg of mutton into the room. ☐
c) He does not know what sort of dog came in. ☐
d) The whole family was in the room when the dog came in. ☐
e) Gosse thinks he learned to speak late because of not hearing other children speaking. ☐
f) When he told this story later other people were amused. ☐
g) Gosse's uncle told people that the child had eaten the mutton. ☐
h) Gosse saw the dog eating the mutton. ☐

Active Learning

Write a short account of one of your earliest memories, making sure that you include at least four pieces of explicit information.

Explicit Information and Ideas 2

Key Technical Skills: Reading

Implicit Information and Ideas 1

Revise 1

Which of the following statements are correct?

a) Implicit information is information that is not directly stated in the text. ☐

b) If something is not directly stated it cannot be true. ☐

c) The writer implies; the reader infers. ☐

d) You can infer something is true by being told something else is not true. ☐

e) 'Imply' and 'infer' mean the same thing. ☐

Revise 2

Read the following sentences.

1. Because I had to leave so early, I skipped breakfast, which is something I hate doing.
2. The taxi driver helped me with my luggage.
3. I was pleased to see the Sydney flight would be leaving on time.
4. I spent the next hours doing anything I could to avoid thinking about flying.

From which of the above sentences can you infer that:

a) The writer does not like flying. ☐

b) The writer travelled by taxi. ☐

c) The writer usually eats breakfast. ☐

d) The writer is going to Australia. ☐

Revise 3

Read the following passage.

> When we bought our bungalow, some thirty years ago, we must have been 500 metres from the cliff edge and nobody mentioned erosion. We just fell in love with the glorious views over the North Sea. It did seem as if the sea was getting a little closer, year by year, but it was a gradual process. I suppose alarm bells should have rung when we found that it was becoming harder to get insurance.
>
> Last year, to celebrate our wedding anniversary, we went on the trip of a lifetime. We took a whole six months to visit our grown-up children, Justin and Lizzie, and their families, in Australia and New Zealand. We had the time of our lives and didn't give a second thought to what was going on in England.

Which of the following can be inferred from the text?

a) The writer is married. ☐
b) The writer lives on the east coast of England. ☐
c) The writer's children live together. ☐
d) The bungalow was the first property the writer ever bought. ☐
e) The insurance companies were concerned about the danger of erosion. ☐
f) The writer was lied to when they bought the bungalow. ☐

Extend

Explain why each statement in Revise 3 either can or can't be inferred from the text.

Active Learning

Look back at the piece of writing you did for the Active Learning exercise on page 7. Re-write it and try to convey the same information but by implication.

Implicit Information and Ideas 1

Key Technical Skills: Reading

Implicit Information and Ideas 2

Revise 1

Which of the following statements imply that the writer enjoyed the journey to Australia, which imply that they didn't enjoy the journey, and which are neutral/give no indication of either feeling?

a) I really looked forward to the journey and I wasn't disappointed. ....

b) The journey lasted over 24 hours. ....

c) By the time I got there I was determined never to set foot on a plane again. ....

d) There was a lovely atmosphere on the plane. ....

e) The seats were too small, the food was dreadful and the other passengers were extremely irritating. ....

Revise 2

What might you infer from the following statements?

a) As soon as I saw Roz I rushed over and threw my arms around her.

....

b) Mark looked nothing like I expected.

....

c) Roz asked after Mum and Dad. I told her they missed her and their grandchildren.

....

Revise 3

Read the following passage and then answer the questions.

> My daughter came home in tears last week because a dinner lady had 'stolen her sweets'! Apparently, this ogress of a jobsworth is employed to stand guard at the entrance to the school canteen and inspect the children's lunch boxes as they enter. If there's anything in there that appears on a list of forbidden foods – sweets, biscuits, sausage rolls, fizzy drinks – she confiscates it. And it seems the headteacher is right behind her; the governors are right behind her; and the government is right behind them. It's called the 'Healthy Schools Initiative' or some such nonsense.

a) What can you infer from the passage about the writer's attitude towards the dinner lady? Support your answer with at least one quotation from the text.

....

....

....

b) What can you infer from the passage about the writer's attitude to the 'Healthy Schools Initiative'? Support your answer with at least one quotation from the text.

....

....

....

Extend

Read the following passage.

> We all love daffodils, don't we? These iconic flowers have come to symbolise everything we associate with the coming of spring – hope, joy, beauty and even re-birth.
>
> The earliest known references to daffodils date from about 300 BC. Their ancestors grew all around the Mediterranean, in present-day Spain and Portugal, and the Middle East. The Greeks and Romans grew daffodils and the Romans, who mistakenly thought they had healing powers, brought them to Britain.
>
> Later, the daffodil fell out of favour with the British and came to be seen as a weed until, in the early 17th century, some gardeners in England started planting daffs in their gardens again. Since then, they have become big business in Britain with tens of thousands bought every spring, especially for Mother's Day and Easter Sunday.

Which of the following statements can be inferred from the text?

a) Daffodils grow in the spring. ☐
b) The Romans preferred daffodils to any other flower. ☐
c) A lot of people buy daffodils for their mothers. ☐
d) British people have always loved daffodils. ☐
e) Daffodils are no longer grown in Spain. ☐
f) Spain and Portugal did not exist as nations in 300 BC. ☐
g) Daffodils have medicinal properties. ☐
h) Daffodils have been written about for over 2000 years. ☐

Active Learning

Use an article from a magazine, newspaper or the internet to make a learning poster about daffodils. On one side, list information explicitly stated in the text. On the other side, list things you can infer.

Key Technical Skills: Reading

Synthesis and Summary 1

Revise 1

Read the following example of the sort of question you would get in question 2 of Paper 2.

> You need to refer to both **Source A** and **Source B** for this question.
>
> The ways the children in the sources spend their school holidays are different.
>
> What can you infer about the differences between the activities enjoyed by both groups of children?

What should you do when answering this question? Tick all the boxes that apply.

a) Write about what you do in the holidays. ☐

b) Write about both texts equally. ☐

c) Use short quotations. ☐

d) Copy out whole sentences from the text. ☐

e) Give your opinion on what the children do. ☐

f) Describe what the children do in your own words. ☐

g) Write about the differences between the children's parents. ☐

h) Comment on the language used by the writers. ☐

i) Focus on the children's activities during the holidays. ☐

j) Spend less than 10 minutes on the question. ☐

Revise 2

Reduce each of the following sentences to five words, giving the essential information without losing sense.

a) One slightly dishevelled child, incredibly, ate six apples.

....

b) Whatever anyone else might say, I like apples and pears.

....

c) Tommy, Mrs O'Donnell's youngest son, fell from a tree.

....

d) Do not, under any circumstances, leave this room.

....

Revise 3

Read the following account of an accident.

> At about four o'clock, Maisie, Tommy, Lucy and John went out into the orchard to play. They were all well-brought-up children and their mother was a very nice lady. That day, she left them to play and went back to the house to have a rest in her magnolia sitting room. The children stayed out for over an hour, playing explorers and pretending they were in the Amazonian jungle. After a while, when Maisie said she was hungry, Tommy said he would climb one of the apple trees and get her an apple, though Lucy protested, saying it would probably make Maisie sick. Maisie was often sick. John said he didn't think the tree was safe. Tommy ignored them and climbed the tree. The best apples were at the end of what looked like a sturdy bough. However, as Tommy inched his way along it, it began to crack. Suddenly, the bough broke. Tommy fell to the ground. He was crying with the pain.

Which **five** of the following pieces of information would be most important in understanding the incident?

a) The children were well–brought–up. ☐
b) The children were playing in the orchard. ☐
c) It was about four o'clock. ☐
d) Mrs O'Donnell's sitting room was magnolia. ☐
e) The children were pretending to be in South America. ☐
f) Tommy climbed the tree to get an apple. ☐
g) Maisie was inclined to be sick. ☐
h) Tommy ignored John's warning. ☐
i) The bough broke while Tommy was on it. ☐
j) Tommy fell to the ground. ☐

Extend

Write a summary of the incident described in Revise 3. Aim for 60 words or fewer.

Active Learning

Write a summary of what you did yesterday in 50 words or fewer.

Key Technical Skills: Reading

Synthesis and Summary 2

Revise 1

Sort these words and phrases into two columns: those you might use to express similarities and those you might use to express differences.

| similarly | both | on the other hand | however | also | but | in contrast |
| in the same way | whereas |

To express similarities	To express differences

Revise 2

Re-read the account of Tommy's accident on page 13. Now read this account of a different incident.

> The children were playing in the back garden, watched by their parents. Jake decided to have a go on the trampoline. Two other children were already there and, as Jake was bouncing up and down, one of them pushed him off the trampoline. He got up laughing and completely unhurt.

Find at least **four** ways in which this incident differs from the first and list them below.

Revise 3

Read the following personal accounts of evenings in the country.

a)
> After tea went to Ambleside – a pleasant cool but not cold evening, Rydale was very beautiful with spear-shaped streaks of polished steel. No letters! – only one newspaper. I returned by Clappersgate. Grasmere was very solemn. In the last glimpse of twilight it calls home the heart to quietness. I had been very melancholy in my walk back. I had many of my saddest thoughts and could not keep the tears within me. But when I came to Grasmere I felt it did me good. I finished my letter to A.H. Ate hasty pudding and went to bed.
>
> (from the diary of Dorothy Wordsworth, 16 May 1800)

b)
> After tea, Mum suggested that we play a board game. There were quite a few in the cottage and we decided on Cluedo. We had one game of it and, frankly, I couldn't see the point. Feeling restless, Jodie and I decided to go for a walk, just down to the village. I have to say it's not a very interesting walk, just a dark lane with hedges either side. When we got there, the shop was open and we bought armfuls of newspapers and magazines, as well as loads of snacks. We had a good laugh with the shopkeeper, which put me in a good mood for the rest of the evening. We stayed up till the early hours, chatting, laughing, reading the gossip magazines and filling up on sweets and crisps.

Find as many differences as you can between the way Dorothy Wordsworth and the writer of the second passage spent their evenings.

Source A	Source B

Extend

Write a summary of the different ways in which the two writers spent their evenings.

Active Learning

Think about two television programmes you have watched, two pieces of music you have listened to or two books you have read. Make a list of the similarities and differences between them.

Key Technical Skills: Reading

Referring to the Text 1

Revise 1

Complete the following statements using the words and phrases below.

a) One way of referring to the text is to .... part of it, putting it in your own words.

b) Direct quotations should always be surrounded by ...., also known as ....

c) Short quotations should be .... in your answer, fitting naturally into the sentence.

d) Longer quotations should be introduced by a ....

| colon | inverted commas | embedded |
| quotation marks | paraphrase | |

Revise 2

Match each direct quotation (**a** to **d**) with its paraphrase (**1** to **4**).

a) He was subjected to no stage of delay, but ushered direct from the door to the dining room where Dr Lanyon sat alone over his wine. ☐

b) I had been very melancholy in my walk back. I had many of my saddest thoughts and could not keep the tears within me. ☐

c) When we got there, the shop was open and we bought armfuls of newspapers and magazines, as well as loads of snacks. ☐

d) My daughter came home in tears last week because a dinner lady had 'stolen her sweets'! ☐

1. The writer's daughter was upset because her sweets were confiscated in school.
2. The writer felt sad while she was walking home and cried.
3. In the shop, the writer bought snacks and reading material.
4. The visitor was quickly taken to see Dr Lanyon, who was drinking in the dining room.

Revise 3

Re-read the following passage from Dorothy Wordsworth's diary.

> After tea went to Ambleside – a pleasant cool but not cold evening, Rydale was very beautiful with spear-shaped streaks of polished steel. No letters! – only one newspaper. I returned by Clappersgate. Grasmere was very solemn. In the last glimpse of twilight it calls home the heart to quietness. I had been very melancholy in my walk back. I had many of my saddest thoughts and could not keep the tears within me. But when I came to Grasmere I felt it did me good. I finished my letter to A.H. Ate hasty pudding and went to bed.

From the passage, pick a short quotation that:

a) describes the weather that evening

b) is a metaphor used to convey the appearance of Rydale

c) describes the writer's mood on the walk home

d) describes the effect of the walk/her crying.

Extend

Write two paragraphs explaining what you learn from the passage above about Dorothy Wordsworth's feelings and how she conveys these feelings. Include all the quotations that you selected for Revise 3.

Active Learning

Look at a practice answer or mock exam you have done in the past. Go through it and improve your use of quotations. You might want to correct the way you have presented them, shorten them, add more or replace them with more appropriate quotations.

Referring to the Text 1

Key Technical Skills: Reading

Referring to the Text 2

Revise 1

a) In the context of referring to a text, what does PEE stand for?

....

b) Explain what each element means in practice:

P ....

E ....

E ....

c) Do you need to use PEE every time you quote from a text? ....

Revise 2

The following passages are all about *A Christmas Carol* by Charles Dickens. Each one should contain at least one quotation from the text. Choose the correct quotation from the box below and insert it in the sentence. You do not need to be familiar with the texts to work out the answers.

a) Belle accuses Scrooge of worshipping money by saying that .... her. An idol is a false god.

b) The simple sentence at the start of the paragraph, ..., does not prepare us for the emotive description of the two creatures that follows it.

c) Adjectives such as .... and .... could paint a violent, dangerous picture, but they are used in the context of a happy family scene.

d) The coldness of his nature is compared to the winter weather:

....

e) The .... where Scrooge's body lies is contrasted with Tiny Tim's room, which is ....

> 'dark, empty house'   'another idol has displaced'   'They were a boy and a girl.'
> 'lighted cheerfully'   'tumultuous'
> 'uproarious'   'The cold within him froze his old features.'

Snap Workbook: Reading

Revise 3

Read the following examples of the use of PEE. Use different colours to highlight the point, the evidence and the explanation.

a) Romeo expresses his love by comparing Juliet to the sun, the moon and the stars: 'It is the east and Juliet is the sun.' This imagery demonstrates that his love is both great and natural.

b) By the end of the novel, Jane and Rochester's relationship has changed dramatically, partly because he has been blinded in the fire. It is almost as if she needs him to be dependent on her for the relationship to work.

c) Snowball, unlike Napoleon, 'is full of plans for innovations and improvements'. These three nouns all have positive connotations, connected with the future.

Extend

Read the following paragraph from *The Sign of Four* by Sir Arthur Conan Doyle. Holmes and Watson have just met Miss Morston. Watson is the narrator of the story.

> I sat in the window with the volume in my hand, but my thoughts were far from the daring speculations of the writer. My mind ran upon our late visitor, – her smiles, the deep rich tones of her voice, the strange mystery which overhung her life. If she were seventeen at the time of her father's disappearance she must be seven-and-twenty now, – a sweet age, when youth has lost its self-consciousness and become a little sobered by experience. So I sat and mused, until such dangerous thoughts came into my head that I hurried away to my desk and plunged furiously into the latest treatise on pathology. What was I, an army surgeon with a weak leg and a weaker bank account, that I should dare to think of such things?

Highlight **three or four** quotations which tell you about Watson's feelings for Miss Morston. Write two or three paragraphs, using these quotations, about the impression you get from this passage of Watson's feelings for Miss Morston.

Active Learning

Looking again at your practice answer or mock exam, check whether you have used PEE. Look especially at 'explain/explore'.

Referring to the Text 2

Key Technical Skills: Reading

Analysing Language 1

Revise 1

Give the correct term for each of the following:

a) A naming word ....

b) A doing, thinking or feeling word ....

c) A word that limits or describes a noun ....

d) A word that limits or describes a verb ....

e) A short word that stands in for another word, usually a noun ....

f) A word used to link a noun, noun phrase or pronoun to another word in the sentence (e.g. to, in)
....

g) A word that joins words, phrases or clauses (e.g. and, because) ....

h) A short word that comes before a noun and helps to define it (e.g. the, some)
....

Revise 2

Read the following paragraph.

> As they approached the burning building, they could see the flames. However, the crew was fully prepared as always. The fire officers unloaded their equipment and sprang into action. Sam was the first to enter the house. Showing great courage, he and Ruby rescued all the children.

Identify and write:

a) Two proper nouns ....

b) Two abstract nouns ....

c) One collective noun ....

d) Six concrete (or common) nouns ....
....
....
....

e) Two pronouns ....

Snap Workbook: Reading

Revise 3

Read the following passage from *The War of the Worlds* by H.G. Wells. Identify the word class (part of speech) of the highlighted words or phrases.

> The artilleryman agreed with me that the house was no place to stay in. He proposed, he said, to make his way Londonward, and thence rejoin his battery – No. 12, of the Horse Artillery. My plan was to return at once to Leatherhead; and so greatly had the strength of the Martians impressed me that I was determined to take my wife to Newhaven, and go with her out of the country forthwith. For I had already perceived clearly that the country about London must inevitably be the scene of a disastrous struggle before such creatures as these could be destroyed.

a) The ....

b) agreed ....

c) My ....

d) and ....

e) strength ....

f) out of ....

g) clearly ....

h) disastrous ....

Extend

Write two paragraphs explaining how Wells uses language to convey the narrator's reaction to the situation he finds himself in. Refer to parts of speech and focus on the connotations of the words you quote, e.g. 'The use of proper nouns such as Newhaven, which refers to a real place, makes the situation seem more real.'

Active Learning

Design and make a learning poster to explain parts of speech/word classes to younger children.

Key Technical Skills: Reading

Analysing Language 2

Revise 1

Indicate which of the following sentences is: **1)** a simple sentence; **2)** a compound sentence; **3)** a complex sentence; or **4)** a minor sentence.

a) Jane had a cup of tea but Arthur drank coffee. ☐

b) He ate two chocolate eclairs. ☐

c) Unbelievable! ☐

d) Although Jane thought he was being quite selfish, she was too polite to say anything. ☐

Revise 2

1. How might you describe the register of the following sentences? Choose from: colloquial, technical, dialectical (written in dialect) and formal.

    a) The lady and gentleman who had just arrived were offered a variety of cream cakes, which had been baked on the premises. _____

    b) I don't know about you, but I could eat meringues till the cows come home.
    _____

    c) Aye, whenever I seen Arthur he was eating the wanes' wee cakes. _____

    d) According to the nutritionist, the eclairs were high in fat and calories and might affect Arthur's cholesterol levels, particularly as he already has a high BMI. _____

2. Referring to the sentences above, find and write:

    a) a modal verb _____

    b) a verb in the passive voice _____

    c) a relative pronoun used as a connective. _____

Revise 3

Read the following paragraph from *Grace*, a short story by James Joyce. A man has been found lying on the floor of the toilets in a Dublin pub.

> His collar was unfastened and his necktie loosed. He opened his eyes for an instant, sighed and closed them again. One of the gentlemen who had carried him upstairs held a dinged silk hat in his hand. The manager asked repeatedly did no one know who the injured man was or where had his friends gone. The door of the bar opened and an immense constable entered. A crowd which had followed him down the laneway collected outside the door, struggling to look through the glass panels.

Identify the following features in the passage:

a) the passive voice

b) a compound sentence

c) indirect speech

d) a relative pronoun used to connect main and subordinate clauses

e) a subordinate clause formed by using a present participle.

Extend

Write two or three paragraphs explaining how Joyce uses language to give a picture of the situation in the pub. You should focus on sentence structure but do not need to limit your comments to sentence structures.

Active Learning

Look at a newspaper or magazine article and highlight or underline examples of simple, compound and complex sentences. Also look for direct and indirect speech.

Key Technical Skills: Reading

Analysing Language 3

Revise 1

The following sentences all include imagery. Complete the table below by indicating whether the imagery is a simile; a metaphor; personification; or pathetic fallacy. In the third column, briefly explain the connotations of the imagery used.

a) All around me, the dark clouds wept tears of anger.

b) She was a seething volcano.

c) He was like a rabbit caught in the headlights.

d) Love conquers all.

	Type of imagery	Connotations
a)		
b)		
c)		
d)		

Revise 2

Read the following paragraph, then complete the table below by writing an example of onomatopoeia, alliteration, assonance and sibilance. In column three, briefly explain the effect of the technique.

> The door clanged behind us. We were trapped. Trapped in a dark, dank, dirty basement. Speaking softly, Sophie reassured me: 'Don't be scared. Go slowly over to the open window. We'll get out easily.'

Technique	Example	Effect
Onomatopoeia		
Alliteration		
Assonance		
Sibilance (also alliteration)		

Snap Workbook: Reading

Revise 3

Read the following paragraph from *Villette* by Charlotte Brontë, then answer the questions below. The narrator, Lucy Snowe, has been living in France but – because of unreturned love – has decided to move on.

> If life be a war, it seemed my destiny to conduct it single-handed. I pondered how to break up my winter-quarters – to leave an encampment where food and forage failed. Perhaps, to effect this change, another pitched battle must be fought with fortune; if so, I had a mind to the encounter: too poor to lose, God might destine me to gain. But what road was open – what plan available?

a) The paragraph is an extended metaphor. To what does the narrator compare her life?

b) What does the use of this metaphor tell us about her feelings about her life?

c) What does the use of the term 'encampment' suggest about her current situation?

d) Identify a use of personification and explain what it says about her attitude.

e) Identify a rhetorical question and explain its effect.

Extend

Using your answers to Revise 3, write two or three paragraphs about how Charlotte Brontë uses language to convey Lucy Snowe's feelings.

Active Learning

Look at a newspaper or magazine article and see how many examples of figurative imagery you can find. Make a learning poster based on them, making the images visual.

Key Technical Skills: Reading

Analysing Language 4

Revise 1

Indicate which rhetorical technique listed below each of the following sentences is an example of.

a) Our achievements will grow and grow over the next year. ....

b) So far, we have been phenomenally and incredibly successful. ....

c) I ask you to do battle with our rivals, silence our critics, and conquer the market place.
....

d) We must rescue our desperate, unloved customers from the bloodthirsty claws of our competitors.
....

e) Do you believe that we can do this together? ....

> rhetorical question   hyperbole   'the rule of three' (triplet)   emotive language   repetition

Revise 2

a) Add verbs, adjectives and adverbs to the following passage to make the reader feel sympathy towards Bertie.

> As .... (adj.), ... (adj.) Bertie walked .... (adv) down the street, he was approached by a .... (adj.), ... (adj.) stranger. .... (adv.), the man .... (verb) money from Bertie. A .... (adj.) Bertie refused to give him anything.

b) Now add verbs, adjectives and adverbs to the same passage to make the reader feel sympathy towards the stranger.

> As .... (adj.), ... (adj.) Bertie walked .... (adv) down the street, he was approached by a .... (adj.), ... (adj.) stranger. .... (adv.), the man .... (verb) money from Bertie. A .... (adj.) Bertie refused to give him anything.

26 Snap Workbook: Reading

> **Revise 3**
>
> Read the following passage, from a speech to a meeting of local residents.
>
> > Last night, less than a mile from where we are sitting now, a frail pensioner was burgled, robbed at knife-point in her own home in a terrifying ordeal. The actions of the burglars are beyond words. However, it is the action – or rather the lack of action – by the police that I worry about. What action did they take? They gave her a leaflet. That's what they did. A vulnerable member of the community, who had shown great courage in fending off ruthless attackers, was given a leaflet about locking her doors at night, installing a burglar alarm and ringing the police. Why on earth would she ring the police? So that they could give her another leaflet?
>
> Use different colours to highlight examples of each of the following:
>
> a) rhetorical question b) emotive language
>
> c) list of three d) hyperbole

> **Extend**
>
> Write two paragraphs explaining the effect of the rhetorical techniques used in the speech above.

> **Active Learning**
>
> Watch the television news and, when politicians are being interviewed, listen for examples of rhetorical techniques.

AS FRAIL, NERVOUS BERTIE WALKED GINGERLY DOWN THE STREET, HE WAS APPROACHED BY A HUGE, TERRIFYING STRANGER. MENACINGLY, THE MAN DEMANDED MONEY FROM BERTIE. A FRIGHTENED BERTIE REFUSED TO GIVE HIM ANYTHING.

AS RICH, ARROGANT BERTIE WALKED CONFIDENTLY DOWN THE STREET, HE WAS APPROACHED BY A NERVOUS, BEDRAGGLED STRANGER. POLITELY, THE MAN BEGGED FOR MONEY FROM BERTIE. A SELFISH BERTIE REFUSED TO GIVE HIM ANYTHING.

Key Technical Skills: Reading

Analysing Form and Structure 1

Revise 1

Below are the opening sentences of some novels. They engage the reader in different ways. Indicate which of them:

a) intrigues the reader by making a seemingly nonsensical statement ☐

b) introduces the protagonist to readers and makes them wonder what his story will be ☐

c) gives the reader some information about the narrator's background ☐

d) introduces the novel's themes in an amusing way. ☐

1. 'My grandmother lived in a handsome house in the clean and ancient town of Bretton.' (*Villette* by Charlotte Brontë)
2. 'It was a bright, cold day in April and the clocks were striking thirteen.' (*1984* by George Orwell)
3. 'It is a truth universally acknowledged that a single man in possession of a good fortune must be in want of a wife.' (*Pride and Prejudice* by Jane Austen)
4. '"I shall never forget Tony's face," said the carrier.' (*Tony Kyte the Arch Deceiver* by Thomas Hardy)

Revise 2

Below are the closing sentences of some novels. Explain the effect of each of the endings.

a) 'Here then, as I lay down my pen, I bring the life of that unhappy Henry Jekyll to an end.' (*The Strange Case of Dr Jekyll and Mr Hyde* by Robert Louis Stevenson)

....

....

b) 'And so, as Tiny Tim observed, "God bless Us, Every One!"' (*A Christmas Carol* by Charles Dickens)

....

....

c) '"O Father," said Eppie, "what a pretty home ours is! I think nobody could be happier than we are."' (*Silas Marner* by George Eliot)

....

....

d) 'He sprang from the cabin window as he said this, upon the ice raft which lay close to the vessel. He was soon borne away by the waves and lost in darkness and distance.' (*Frankenstein* by Mary Shelley)

....

....

Revise 3

Read the following passage, the opening paragraph of *A Ramble in Aphasia*, a short story by O. Henry, and then answer the questions below.

> My wife and I parted on that morning in precisely our usual manner. She left her second cup of tea to follow me to the front door. There she plucked from my lapel the invisible strand of lint (the universal act of woman to proclaim ownership) and bade me take care of my cold. I had no cold. Next came her kiss of parting – the level kiss of domesticity flavoured with Young Hyson[1]. There was no fear of the extemporaneous[2], of variety spicing her infinite custom. With the deft touch of long malpractice, she dabbed awry my well-set scarf pin; and then, as I closed the door, I heard her morning slippers pattering back to her cooling tea.
>
> [1] A type of Chinese green tea. [2] spontaneous or unprepared

a) What do we learn about the narrator from the first line?

b) What impression do you get of his wife?

c) How do you think he feels about his marriage?

d) Find two phrases which suggest that the marriage has become boring.

e) Find two phrases which suggest his irritation with his wife.

f) How do you think the story might develop?

Extend

Write two paragraphs about how Henry uses his opening paragraph to interest the reader in his story.

Active Learning

Find the text of 'A Ramble in Aphasia' on the internet. Read the rest of the story (it's quite short!) and think about how the story has either fulfilled your expectations or surprised you.

Key Technical Skills: Reading

Analysing Form and Structure 2

Revise 1

Put the following sentences into chronological order:

a) He discussed his ideas with the others over lunch. ☐

b) Early on Sunday morning, Frankie decided it was time for action. ☐

c) However, he spent a restless night wondering whether they had made the right decisions. ☐

d) By evening their plans were complete. ☐

e) By the time he got up on Monday, he had completely changed his mind. ☐

Revise 2

Explain the following terms.

a) flashback

....
....

b) 'big to small' structure

....
....

c) circular structure

....
....

d) reverse chronological order

....
....

Revise 3

Read the following passage from *The Withered Arm* by Thomas Hardy and then answer the questions below.

> The road from Anglebury to Holmstoke is in general level; but there is one place where a sharp ascent breaks the monotony. Farmers homeward-bound from the former market-town who trot all the rest of the way, walk their horses up this short incline.
>
> The next evening while the sun was yet bright a handsome new gig[1], with a lemon-coloured body and red wheels, was spinning westward along the level highway at the heels of a powerful mare. The driver was a yeoman in the prime of life, cleanly shaven like an actor, his face being toned to that bluish-vermillion hue which so often graces a thriving farmer's features when returning home after successful dealings in the town. Beside him sat a woman, many years his junior – almost, indeed, a girl. Her face too was fresh in colour, but it was of a totally different quality – soft and evanescent, like the light under a heap of rose petals.
>
> [1] a light, two-wheeled carriage, pulled by horses

a) This passage comes at the beginning of the second chapter. Identify the discourse marker Hardy uses to show the passing of time from the previous chapter.

b) What is the purpose of the short first paragraph?

c) How does Hardy change focus between the first and second paragraphs?

d) How does he change his focus during the course of the second paragraph?

Extend

How does Hardy interest his readers in the couple in the gig? Make sure that you refer to structure in your answer.

Active Learning

Read *The Withered Arm* by Thomas Hardy (you should be able to find it online) and think about how Hardy has structured the whole story.

Analysing Form and Structure 2

English Language — Creative Reading 1

Revise 1

Which of the following statements about the reading section of the exam paper are true?

a) You are advised to spend 15 minutes reading the source material and questions before you start to write. ☐

b) You should not write on the exam paper. ☐

c) The second question focuses on language. ☐

d) In question 2 you should comment on sentence forms, language features and techniques. ☐

e) You should write about language techniques in your answer to question 3. ☐

f) Question 3 is about the structure of the extract. ☐

g) You will be rewarded for using subject terminology accurately. ☐

h) In answering question 1 you should tick only one box per part. ☐

i) You should refer to the extract in all your answers. ☐

j) You will get extra marks for neat handwriting. ☐

Revise 2

Match these terms to the correct definitions:

a) protagonist ☐

b) resolution or denouement ☐

c) antagonist ☐

d) exposition ☐

e) turning point ☐

f) inciting incident ☐

g) climax ☐

1. something that happens to change things and get the story started
2. the main character
3. a point in the narrative where things change
4. the high point of the action from which there is no return
5. a character who opposes the main character
6. the opening of the story, establishing the 'world' of the story and giving some background
7. the end of the story, when things are sorted out and a conclusion reached

Snap Workbook: Reading

Revise 3

Read the following passage, the opening of the short story *The Boarding House* by James Joyce. The story takes place in Dublin in the late 19th to early 20th century.

> Mrs Mooney was a butcher's daughter. She was a woman who was quite able to keep things to herself: a determined woman. She had married her father's foreman and opened a butcher's shop near Spring Gardens. But as soon as his father-in-law was dead Mr Mooney started to go to the devil. He drank, plundered the till, ran headlong into debt. It was no use making him take the pledge: he was sure to break out again a few days after. By fighting his wife in the presence of customers and by buying bad meat he ruined his business. One night he went for his wife with the cleaver and she had to sleep in a neighbour's house.

Tick (✓) one box for each question.

a) What did Mrs Mooney's father do for a living?

- He was a soldier ☐
- He was a businessman ☐
- He was a butcher ☐

b) What is Mrs Mooney like?

- Determined ☐
- Lazy ☐
- Timid ☐

c) Which of these things does Mr Mooney not do?

- Get into debt ☐
- Have affairs with other women ☐
- Drink too much ☐

d) How does Mrs Mooney escape from her husband?

- She goes and sleeps in a neighbour's house ☐
- She attacks him with a cleaver ☐
- She goes back to her father ☐

Extend

Look again at the passage above. Identify the protagonist, the antagonist and the inciting incident. Give reasons for your answers.

Active Learning

Look up specimen questions and past papers for English Language Paper 1. Study the reading questions to ensure that you are familiar with the format and requirements of them.

Creative Reading 1

English Language — Creative Reading 2

Revise 1

Match these terms to the correct definitions:

a) a first-person narrative ☐

b) a third-person narrative ☐

c) an omniscient narrator ☐

d) an intrusive narrator ☐

e) a reliable first-person narrator ☐

f) an unreliable narrator ☐

g) a naïve narrator ☐

1. any narrative where the narrator is not involved in the action
2. a narrator telling his or her own story who can be trusted by the reader
3. a writer who interrupts the narrative to express his or her own thoughts
4. a narrator whose account may be incomplete because he or she does not know the whole story
5. a narrator who might mislead the reader
6. a narrator who is outside the action and knows all the characters' thoughts and feelings
7. any narrative where the narrator tells his or her own story (using 'I')

Revise 2

Identify the kind of narrator used by the writers of the following extracts:

a) He then asked her to marry him. Sophy did not exactly love him, but she had respect for him which almost amounted to veneration. (*The Son's Veto* by Thomas Hardy)

b) I remember how mockingly bright the day seemed as I went back on my melancholy pilgrimage to the little house in Woking, how busy the streets and how vivid the moving life about me. (*The War of the Worlds* by H.G. Wells)

c) I suppose one reason why we are seldom able to comfort our neighbours with our words is that our goodwill gets adulterated, in spite of ourselves, before it can pass our lips. (*Silas Marner* by George Eliot)

Snap Workbook: Reading

Revise 3

This passage from *The Boarding House* by James Joyce follows on from the extract on page 33. Read the extract and then answer the questions below.

> After that they lived apart. She went to the priest and got a separation from him with care of the children. She would give him neither money nor food nor house-room; and so he was obliged to enlist himself as a sheriff's man. He was a shabby stooped little drunkard with a white face and a white moustache, white eyebrows, pencilled above his little eyes, which were veined and raw; and all day long he sat in the bailiff's room, waiting to be put on a job. Mrs Mooney, who had taken what remained of her money out of the butcher business and set up a boarding house in Hardwicke Street, was a big imposing woman. Her house had a floating population made up of tourists from Liverpool and the Isle of Man and, occasionally, artistes from the music halls. Its resident population was made up of clerks from the city. She governed the house cunningly and firmly, knew when to give credit, when to be stern and when to let things pass. All the resident young men spoke of her as The Madam.

a) What sort of narrator does Joyce use here?

b) Find two adjectives used to describe Mr Mooney and explain their effect.

c) Find two adverbs used to describe Mrs Mooney's behaviour and explain their effect.

d) Give an example of repetition and explain its effect.

Extend

How does Joyce, as the omniscient narrator, introduce the setting and characters to the reader? Think about:

- what we learn about the characters and setting
- how Joyce uses structure and language to introduce characters and setting.

Active Learning

Make a learning poster showing different types of narrator, with examples from books you have read.

English Language — Creative Reading 3

Revise 1

Look at the following description of Amy from *Little Women* by Louisa May Alcott.

> Amy, though the youngest, was the most important person – in her own opinion at least. A regular snow-maiden, with blue eyes, and yellow hair, curling on her shoulders, pale and slender, and always carrying herself like a young lady mindful of her manners.

Which of the following things do we learn about Amy? Tick the **four** correct answers.

a) she is the youngest in the family ☐
b) she is very tall ☐
c) she is blonde and pale ☐
d) she is clever ☐
e) she is self-centred ☐
f) she is well-mannered ☐
g) she is aggressive ☐
h) she is lonely ☐

Revise 2

Read the quotations in the table below, taken from *Silas Marner* by George Eliot.

In the second column, enter how we learn about the character of Silas Marner, choosing from:

a) Narrator's description
b) What the character says
c) What other characters say to or about him
d) What the character does
e) How others feel about him.

In the third column, briefly explain what we learn about the character.

Quotation	How we learn about Silas Marner	What we learn about Silas Marner
Again he put his trembling hands to his head, and gave a wild ringing scream, the cry of desolation.		
He was believed to be a young man of exemplary life and ardent faith.		
He was then simply a pallid young man, with prominent, short-sighted brown eyes.		

Snap Workbook: Reading

'Robbed!' said Silas gaspingly. 'I've been robbed! I want the constable and the Justice – and Squire Cass – and Mr Crackenthorp.'		
'And he's took care of me and loved me from the first, and I'll cleave to him as long as he lives, and nobody shall ever come between him and me.' (Eppie)		

Revise 3

Read the following description of Jo from *Little Women* by Louisa May Alcott and then answer the questions below. Support each answer with at least one short quotation.

> Fifteen-year-old Jo was very tall, thin and brown, and reminded one of a colt; for she never seemed to know what to do with her long limbs, which were very much in her way. She had a decided mouth, a comical nose, and sharp, grey eyes, which appeared to see everything, and were by turns fierce, funny or thoughtful. Her long, thick hair was her one beauty; but it was usually bundled in a net, to be out of her way. Round shoulders had Jo, big hands and feet, a fly-away look to her clothes, and the uncomfortable appearance of a girl who was rapidly shooting up into a woman.

a) How would you summarise Jo's appearance?

b) What do you learn about Jo's character from the description?

Extend

Write two or three paragraphs exploring how Louisa May Alcott uses language to give a first impression of Jo. You could include the writer's use of words and phrases, language features and techniques, and sentence forms.

Active Learning

Look online for images of actresses playing Jo and Amy in film adaptations of *Little Women*. Do you think they are faithful to Alcott's descriptions?

English Language — Creative Reading 4

Revise 1

Which of the following statements about question 4 in the reading section of the exam are true?

a) You must agree with the statement made in the question. ☐

b) You should comment on the writer's use of language and structure. ☐

c) You must refer to the text. ☐

d) You will be rewarded for using subject terminology accurately. ☐

e) The examiners want to know about the effect the text has on you. ☐

f) There is only one right answer. ☐

Revise 2

Match the five quotations below to the five descriptions of the writers' use of language.

a) Fortune suddenly smiled on Jo and dropped a good luck penny in her lap.
   (*Little Women* by Louisa May Alcott) ☐

b) 'Ay, my dear, I did ask ye – to be sure I did, now I think of it – but I had quite forgot it.'
   (*Tony Kytes the Arch-deceiver* by Thomas Hardy) ☐

c) The planet Mars, I scarcely need remind the reader, revolves about the sun at a mean distance of 140,000,000 miles, and the light and heat it receives from the sun is barely half of that received by this world. (*The War of the Worlds* by H.G. Wells) ☐

d) Alan, leaping back to get his distance, ran upon the others like a bull, roaring as he went.
   (*Kidnapped* by Robert Louis Stevenson) ☐

e) Then why should not Eleanor Harding be attached to John Bold?
   (*The Warden* by Anthony Trollope) ☐

1. The writer uses a simile to convey the nature and impact of the character's action.

2. The writer uses non-Standard English in direct speech to suggest the character's class and regional origins.

3. The writer uses personification, making an idea seem more real by writing about it as if it were a person interacting with the character.

4. The intrusive narrator uses a rhetorical question to involve the reader in the fate of the characters.

5. The first-person narrator uses what appears to be scientific fact to convince the reader that he is a reliable witness to the events he will describe.

Revise 3

Read the following extract from *The Boarding House* by James Joyce, which follows on from the extract on page 35.

> Jack Mooney, the Madam's son, who was clerk to a commission agent in Fleet Street, had the reputation of being a hard case. He was fond of using soldiers' obscenities: usually he came home in the small hours. When he met his friends he had always a good one to tell them and he was always sure to be on to a good thing – that is to say, a likely horse or a likely artiste. He was also handy with the mits and sang comic songs. On Sunday nights there would often be a reunion in Mrs Mooney's front drawing-room. The music-hall artistes would oblige; and Sheridan played waltzes and polkas and vamped accompaniments. Polly Mooney, the Madam's daughter, would also sing. She sang:
>
> > I'm a ... naughty girl.
> > You needn't sham:
> > You know I am.
>
> Polly was a slim girl of nineteen; she had light soft hair and a small full mouth. Her eyes, which were grey with a shade of green through them, had a habit of glancing upwards when she spoke with anyone, which made her look like a little perverse madonna. Mrs Mooney had first sent her daughter to be a typist in a corn-factor's office but, as a disreputable sheriff's man used to come every other day to the office, asking to be allowed to say a word to his daughter, she had taken her daughter home again and set her to do housework. As Polly was very lively the intention was to give her the run of the young men. Besides young men like to feel that there is a young woman not very far away. Polly, of course, flirted with the young men but Mrs Mooney, who was a shrewd judge, knew that the young men were only passing the time away: none of them meant business. Things went on so for a long time and Mrs Mooney began to think of sending Polly back to typewriting when she noticed that something was going on between Polly and one of the young men. She watched the pair and kept her own counsel.

Briefly explain:

a) the impression you get of Jack Mooney

b) the impression you get of Polly Mooney

c) the impression you get of Mrs Mooney's attitude to her children.

Extend

Write two or three paragraphs in response to this statement:

'In this part of the story, Mrs Mooney shows very different attitudes to her two children's behaviour. Her response to Polly is intriguing and ambiguous.'

Active Learning

Read the rest of *The Boarding House* (you should find it easily online) to see how the story develops.

English Language — Reading Non-fiction 1

Revise 1

Which of the following statements about the Paper 2 reading section of the exam are true?

a) You should spend 15 minutes reading the sources and the questions before starting to write. ☐

b) You can pick which source to write about. ☐

c) For two of the questions you need to compare the two sources. ☐

d) You should comment on presentation. ☐

e) Not all the questions carry the same number of marks. ☐

f) For questions 1 and 3 you refer to only one source. ☐

g) You should comment on the writer's use of language for question 2. ☐

h) You should comment on the writer's use of language for question 3. ☐

i) You should refer closely to the text when answering questions 2 to 4. ☐

j) You should fill in all the boxes below question 1. ☐

Revise 2

a) Give three examples of non-fiction forms you might be asked to write about.
   ....
   ....

b) Give three examples of writers' possible purposes in writing non-fiction.
   ....
   ....

c) Explain what is meant by writers' 'viewpoints and perspectives'.
   ....
   ....

Revise 3

Look at the following passage from a travel guide to the Italian Lakes.

> Lake Garda, Italy's largest lake, is a beautiful expanse of blue, originally created by glaciation. The breath-taking scenery varies from dramatic snow-capped mountains to tranquil sandy shores and softly undulating vine-covered hills. This area has inspired countless poets and painters from Roman times to the present day. Now Lake Garda is fast becoming one of Italy's most popular tourist destinations, an ideal spot for walking, water sports, or simply relaxing in the Italian sun.

Choose **four** statements below which are true.

a) Lake Garda is Italy's largest lake. ☐

b) Wine is not grown in the region. ☐

c) The writer finds Lake Garda boring. ☐

d) Lake Garda is a popular tourist destination. ☐

e) According to the writer, the area has inspired poets and painters. ☐

f) Nobody knows how the lake was formed. ☐

g) Some tourists enjoy walking in the region. ☐

h) Garda is the capital of Italy. ☐

Extend

Look again at the passage above about Lake Garda. Write a paragraph or two exploring how the writer tries to persuade the reader that Lake Garda is worth visiting.

Active Learning

Find a travel brochure or a website about somewhere you'd like to visit. Try to find five useful pieces of information in it.

English Language — Reading Non-fiction 2

Revise 1

Match the following forms of non-fiction writing to the descriptions below.

a) Letter to a newspaper ☐
b) Travel writing ☐
c) Opinion piece or editorial in a newspaper ☐
d) Article in a magazine for teenagers ☐
e) Autobiography ☐

1. An account of the writer's own life.
2. A book or article about the writer's experience of different places.
3. An article that gives a journalist's point of view on a topical issue.
4. A piece that is intended to entertain, inform and maybe give a point of view to a young audience.
5. The viewpoint or perspective of a reader on a topical issue or an article he or she has read.

Revise 2

Complete the following paragraph, using the words given below.

While some writers of **(a)** _____ in newspapers and magazines use them as a platform to express strongly held **(b)** _____, others prefer to write about the trials and tribulations of everyday life. They tend to start with an **(c)** _____, often about a member of their family doing something which the writer finds amusing and describes using **(d)** _____ and sentimental **(e)** _____ (The lamb! The angel!). Personally, I find most of these trivial ramblings a complete waste of print. And I know that if I were the son or daughter of one these so-called **(f)** _____, I would absolutely forbid my parent from writing anything about me ever and, if they ignored me, I would gain revenge by writing a **(g)** _____ newspaper article from the child's **(h)** _____, full of **(i)** _____ tricks (How could you do this to me?), **(j)** _____ language (I will never recover from your betrayal!) and devastating wit – at the parent's expense of course.

| anecdote | imagery | perspective | hyperbolic | opinion pieces | views | cliched |
| rhetorical | journalists | heartfelt | | | | |

Snap Workbook: Reading

> **Revise 3**

Read the following extract from *Pictures from Italy* by Charles Dickens.

> One of the rottenest-looking parts of the town, I think, is down by the landing-wharf: though it may be, that its being associated with rottenness on the evening of our arrival, has stamped it deeper in my mind. Here, again, the houses are very high, and are of an infinite variety of deformed shapes, and have … something hanging out of a great many windows, and wafting its frowsy[1] fragrance on the breeze. Sometimes, it is a curtain; sometimes, it is a carpet; sometimes, it is a bed; sometimes, a whole line-full of clothes; but there is almost always something.
>
> [1] dingy, musty, unkempt

a) How does Dickens make it clear that he is expressing a personal viewpoint?

b) What metaphor does Dickens use to express the impact the scene made on him? Explain its effect.

c) Find three examples of negative diction and explain the effect on the reader.

d) Find an example of repetition (anaphora) and explain its effect.

> **Extend**

Building on your answers to Revise 3, explain how Dickens uses language to convey the impression the town has made on him.

> **Active Learning**

Have another look at your travel brochure or website. Make a note of the language techniques the writers use to persuade the reader to visit the destination.

English Language — Reading Non-fiction 3

Revise 1

In answering question 2 of Paper 2, which of the following would it be appropriate to comment on? Tick four correct answers.

a) The connotations of the language used ☐

b) The headline ☐

c) A photograph used to illustrate the text ☐

d) The writer's name ☐

e) The use of sentence structures ☐

f) The use of rhetorical devices ☐

g) Whether or not you agree with what the writer says ☐

h) Another text ☐

Revise 2

Below are four sentences followed by comments a student might make about them. Match the sentences to the comments.

a) According to the 2021 census, more than 20% of British people live alone. ☐

b) Not only is this exploitation of natural resources completely destroying our health, it will undoubtedly lead to the total destruction of our planet within a generation. ☐

c) Local resident Joan Lascelles told me that, since the new road was built, the area had 'gone right down' and life in the village was 'turning into a horror story'. ☐

d) It would mean a great deal to a lot of people if the government could make this a priority. ☐

1. The writer quotes another person's point of view without comment.
2. The writer uses statistics and cites a source to make the statement credible.
3. The writer uses modal verbs to create a polite and reasonable tone.
4. The writer uses hyperbole in expressing a strongly held view.

Revise 3

Read the following two accounts of childhood holidays. Find **five** differences between them.

Source A: We went every year to my parents' house in France. It was certainly luxurious, with its own swimming pool and every modern facility imaginable. It was set in beautiful countryside and we had everything we could wish for. Berthe and Arnaud, a lovely local couple, waited on us hand and foot, doing everything from baking fresh croissants to cleaning out the pool. But I have to admit, I never really enjoyed those holidays. I was an only child and, with no other children in the neighbourhood, I was bored.

Source B: Every year the whole family went camping in Dorset. It was a bit rough and ready. I certainly wasn't keen on the shared toilet facilities, though my mother kept telling us 'it could be worse, it could be a hole in the ground'. And we all had to, in her words, 'muck in': walking miles to the shop, building a fire, cooking, cleaning. However, looking back, they were the best holidays I ever had. As well as the six of us, there were loads of other children on the campsite and we were certainly never bored.

Source A	Source B

Extend

Building on your answer to Revise 3, write a paragraph or two about the differences between the holidays described in the two sources.

Active Learning

Try re-writing the two paragraphs above about holidays so that the first has a positive tone and the second has a negative tone.

Reading Non-fiction 3

English Language — Reading Non-fiction 4

Revise 1

Which of the following statements about question 4 in the reading section of the exam are true?

a) You should plan to spend more time on this answer than on any of the previous three. ☐

b) You are allowed to write about just one of the sources. ☐

c) The question will focus on a particular aspect of the sources. ☐

d) You should comment on the writer's use of language and structure. ☐

e) You must refer to the text. ☐

f) You will be rewarded for using subject terminology accurately. ☐

g) You should comment on the differing attitudes/viewpoints of the writers. ☐

h) Your answer should focus on your own point of view. ☐

Revise 2

Look at these two reviews of the same show.

Review A: The audience was standing and cheering at the end of this show and the ovation was well-deserved. It was a triumph from start to finish. This all-new production of *Oliver* by local company The Vagabonds makes the well-known story seem fresh and relevant. Tom Brown's truly menacing Fagin slavers like a hungry wolf in his scenes with young Julian Forbes-Smith's Oliver, and the other members of the cast are almost faultless. Don't miss it!

Review B: I really have to take issue with the current trend for audiences to leap to their feet at the end of every mediocre production. I know they're amateurs and, no doubt, they were trying hard but, frankly, this production of *Oliver* was dire from start to finish. It went on far too long and offered no insights into what is already a tired and cliché-ridden script. I will draw a veil over the performances. To comment on them in detail would be cruel.

Across the two reviews, find and write an example of:

a) an imperative to encourage readers to see the show ....

b) a simile to describe an effective performance ....

c) a metaphor to express dislike of the performances ....

d) use of the first person to give a conversational tone ....

Revise 3

Re-read the passages on pages 41 (the travel guide about Lake Garda) and 43 (*Pictures from Italy*). Answer the questions in the table below.

	Text A (Lake Garda travel guide)	Text B (*Pictures from Italy*)
What is the writer's attitude to the place?		
What is the purpose of the text?		
How would you describe the general tone of the piece?		
Comment on the writer's use of sentence structures.		
Comment on the writer's use of language features		

Extend

Building on your answers to Revise 3, write two or three paragraphs comparing how the writers convey their different feelings and perspectives.

Active Learning

Look up specimen questions and past papers for English Language Paper 2. Study the reading questions to ensure that you are familiar with the format and requirements of them.

Exam Practice

Paper 1, Reading 1

Spend about 15 minutes reading the source material below and the four questions on pages 49–50.

This extract is the opening of a short story, *The Odour of Chrysanthemums* by D.H. Lawrence, first published in 1914. It is set in a Nottinghamshire mining town.

The small locomotive engine, Number 4, came clanking, stumbling down from Selston – with seven full waggons. It appeared round the corner with loud threats of speed, but the colt that it startled from among the gorse, which still flickered indistinctly in the raw afternoon, outdistanced it at a canter. A woman, walking up the railway line to Underwood, drew back into the hedge, held her basket aside, and watched the footplate of the engine advancing. The trucks thumped heavily past, one by one, with slow inevitable movement, as she stood insignificantly trapped between the jolting black waggons and the hedge; then they curved away towards the coppice where the withered oak leaves dropped noiselessly, while the birds, pulling at the scarlet hips beside the track, made off into the dusk that had already crept into the spinney. In the open, the smoke from the engine sank and cleaved to the rough grass. The fields were dreary and forsaken, and in the marshy strip that led to the whimsey, a reedy pit-pond, the fowls had already abandoned their run among the alders, to roost in the tarred fowl-house. The pit-bank loomed up beyond the pond, flames like red sores licking its ashy sides, in the afternoon's stagnant light. Just beyond rose the tapering chimneys and the clumsy black head-stocks of Brinsley Colliery. The two wheels were spinning fast up against the sky, and the winding-engine rapped out its little spasms. The miners were being turned up.

The engine whistled as it came into the wide bay of railway lines beside the colliery, where rows of trucks stood in harbour.

Miners, single, trailing and in groups, passed like shadows diverging home. At the edge of the ribbed level of sidings squat a low cottage, three steps down from the cinder track. A large bony vine clutched at the house, as if to claw down the tiled roof. Round the bricked yard grew a few wintry primroses. Beyond, the long garden sloped down to a bush-covered brook course. There were some twiggy apple trees, winter-crack trees, and ragged cabbages. Beside the path hung dishevelled pink chrysanthemums, like pink cloths hung on bushes. A woman came stooping out of the felt-covered fowl-house, half-way down the garden. She closed and padlocked the door, then drew herself erect, having brushed some bits from her white apron.

She was a tall woman of imperious mien, handsome, with definite black eyebrows. Her smooth black hair was parted exactly. For a few moments she stood steadily watching the miners as they passed along the railway: then she turned towards the brook course. Her face was calm and set, her mouth was closed with disillusionment. After a moment she called:

'John!' There was no answer. She waited, and then said distinctly:

'Where are you?'

'Here!' replied a child's sulky voice from among the bushes. The woman looked piercingly through the dusk.

'Are you at that brook?' she asked sternly.

For answer the child showed himself before the raspberry-canes that rose like whips. He was a small, sturdy boy of five. He stood quite still, defiantly.

'Oh!' said the mother, conciliated. 'I thought you were down at that wet brook – and you remember what I told you –'

The boy did not move or answer.

'Come, come on in,' she said more gently, 'it's getting dark. There's your grandfather's engine coming down the line!'

Question 1

Re-read the first part of the source, from lines 1 to 5 (to '... the engine advancing.').

Tick (✓) one box for each question.

a) What size is the train?

- Small ☐
- Medium ☐
- Long ☐

b) What is the engine pulling?

- Seven full waggons ☐
- A colt ☐
- A load of gorse ☐

c) How do we know the train is moving slowly?

- It cannot outpace the woman ☐
- The woman is able to watch it ☐
- A cantering colt is faster ☐

d) What runs along the side of the track?

- A road ☐
- A hedge ☐
- A river ☐

(4 marks)

Question 2

Look in detail at the following extract from lines 5 to 15 of the source.

> The trucks thumped heavily past, one by one, with slow inevitable movement, as she stood insignificantly trapped between the jolting black waggons and the hedge; then they curved away towards the coppice where the withered oak leaves dropped noiselessly, while the birds, pulling at the scarlet hips beside the track, made off into the dusk that had already crept into the spinney. In the open, the smoke from the engine sank and cleaved to the rough grass. The fields were dreary and forsaken, and in the marshy strip that led to the whimsey, a reedy pit-pond, the fowls had already abandoned their run among the alders, to roost in the tarred fowl-house. The pit-bank loomed up beyond the pond, flames like red sores licking its ashy sides, in the afternoon's stagnant light. Just beyond rose the tapering chimneys and the clumsy black head-stocks of Brinsley Colliery. The two wheels were spinning fast up against the sky, and the winding-engine rapped out its little spasms. The miners were being turned up.

How does the writer use language here to describe the scene as the train approaches the town?

You could include the writer's choice of:

- words and phrases
- language features and techniques
- sentence forms.

(8 marks)

Question 3

You now need to think about the whole of the source.

The text is from the opening of a story.

How has the writer structured the text to create a sense of place?

You could write about:

- how the writer focuses your attention on the setting at the beginning
- how the writer uses structure to create effects
- the writer's use of any other structural features, such as changes in mood, tone or perspective.

(8 marks)

Question 4

Focus this part of your answer on the second half of the source from line 16 ('The engine whistled ...') to the end.

In this part of the story, the writer effectively introduces a complex character and her environment.

To what extent do you agree or disagree with this statement?

In your response you could:

- write about your own impressions of the woman and her environment
- comment on how the writer has created these impressions
- support your response with references to the text.

(20 marks)

Exam Practice — Paper 1, Reading 2

Spend about 15 minutes reading the source material below and the four questions on pages 52–53.

This extract is from a short story, *The Bull* by H.H. Munro (Saki), first published in 1914. Farmer Tom Yorkfield has taken his half-brother Laurence, who is an artist, to see his prize bull.

Tom had done his best, with the little capital at his command, to maintain and improve the standard of his small herd of cattle, and in Clover Fairy he had bred a bull which was something rather better than any that his immediate neighbours could show. It would not have made a sensation in the judging-ring at an important cattle show, but it was as vigorous, shapely, and
5 healthy a young animal as any small practical farmer could wish to possess. At the King's Head on market days Clover Fairy was very highly spoken of, and Yorkfield used to declare that he would not part with him for a hundred pounds; a hundred pounds is a lot of money in the small farming line, and probably anything over eighty would have tempted him.

It was with some especial pleasure that Tom took advantage of one of Laurence's rare visits to
10 the farm to lead him down to the enclosure where Clover Fairy kept solitary state – the grass widower of a grazing harem. Tom felt some of his old dislike for his half-brother reviving; the artist was becoming more languid in his manner, more unsuitably turned-out in attire, and he seemed inclined to impart a slightly patronising tone to his conversation. He took no heed of a flourishing potato crop, but waxed enthusiastic over a clump of yellow-flowering weed that stood
15 in a corner by a gateway, which was rather galling to the owner of a really very well weeded farm; again, when he might have been duly complimentary about a group of fat, black-faced lambs, that simply cried aloud for admiration, he became eloquent over the foliage tints of an oak copse on the hill opposite. But now he was being taken to inspect the crowning pride and glory of Helsery; however grudging he might be in his praises, however backward and niggardly with his
20 congratulations, he would have to see and acknowledge the many excellences of that redoubtable animal. Some weeks ago, while on a business journey to Taunton, Tom had been invited by his half-brother to visit a studio in that town, where Laurence was exhibiting one of his pictures, a large canvas representing a bull standing knee-deep in some marshy ground; it had been good of its kind, no doubt, and Laurence had seemed inordinately pleased with it; 'the best thing I've
25 done yet,' he had said over and over again, and Tom had generously agreed that it was fairly life-like. Now, the man of pigments was going to be shown a real picture, a living model of strength and comeliness, a thing to feast the eyes on, a picture that exhibited new pose and action with every shifting minute, instead of standing glued into one unvarying attitude between the four walls of a frame. Tom unfastened a stout wooden door and led the way into a straw-bedded yard.

30 'Is he quiet?' asked the artist, as a young bull with a curly red coat came inquiringly towards them.

'He's playful at times,' said Tom, leaving his half-brother to wonder whether the bull's ideas of play were of the catch-as-catch-can order. Laurence made one or two perfunctory comments on the animal's appearance and asked a question or so as to his age and such-like details; then he
35 coolly turned the talk into another channel.

'Do you remember the picture I showed you at Taunton?' he asked.

'Yes,' grunted Tom; 'a white-faced bull standing in some slush. Don't admire those Herefords much myself; bulky-looking brutes, don't seem to have much life in them. Daresay they're easier to paint that way; now, this young beggar is on the move all the time, aren't you, Fairy?'

40 'I've sold that picture,' said Laurence, with considerable complacency in his voice.

'Have you?' said Tom; 'glad to hear it, I'm sure. Hope you're pleased with what you've got for it.'

'I got three hundred pounds for it,' said Laurence.

Tom turned towards him with a slowly rising flush of anger in his face. Three hundred pounds! Under the most favourable market conditions that he could imagine his prized Clover Fairy
45 would hardly fetch a hundred, yet here was a piece of varnished canvas, painted by his half-brother, selling for three times that sum. It was a cruel insult that went home with all the more force because it emphasised the triumph of the patronising, self-satisfied Laurence.

Question 1

Re-read the first part of the source, from lines 1 to 8 (to '... tempted him.').

Tick (✓) one box for each question.

a) How does Tom's bull compare with those of his neighbours?

It is almost as good ☐

It is rather better ☐

It is sensational ☐

b) What are the bull's strong points?

It is vigorous, shapely and healthy ☐

It has won prizes at important cattle shows ☐

It is agile and highly intelligent ☐

c) Where do people speak well of the bull?

Important cattle shows ☐

The King's Head pub ☐

The local market ☐

d) What amount of money might persuade Tom to sell his bull?

Anything over £80 ☐

£100 ☐

Anything over £100 ☐

(4 marks)

Question 2

Look in detail at the following extract, from lines 9 to 21 of the source.

> It was with some especial pleasure that Tom took advantage of one of Laurence's rare visits to the farm to lead him down to the enclosure where Clover Fairy kept solitary state – the grass widower of a grazing harem. Tom felt some of his old dislike for his half-brother reviving; the artist was becoming more languid in his manner, more unsuitably turned-out in attire, and he seemed inclined to impart a slightly patronising tone to his conversation. He took no heed of a flourishing potato crop, but waxed enthusiastic over a clump of yellow-flowering weed that stood in a corner by a gateway, which was rather galling to the owner of a really very well weeded farm; again, when he might have been duly complimentary about a group of fat, black-faced lambs, that simply cried aloud for admiration, he became eloquent over the foliage tints of an oak copse on the hill opposite. But now he was being taken to inspect the crowning pride and glory of Helsery; however grudging he might be in his praises, however backward and niggardly with his congratulations, he would have to see and acknowledge the many excellences of that redoubtable animal.

How does the writer use language here to describe Tom and Laurence's walk?

You could include the writer's choice of:

- words and phrases
- language features and techniques
- sentence forms.

(8 marks)

Question 3

You now need to think about the whole of the source.

The text is from a short story.

How has the writer structured the text to create a sense of the difference between the two brothers?

You could write about:

- what the writer focuses your attention on at the beginning of this extract
- how the writer contrasts the brothers
- the writer's use of any other structural features, such as changes in mood, tone or perspective.

(8 marks)

Question 4

Focus this part of your answer on the second part of the source, from line 21 ('Some weeks ago …') to the end.

In this part of the story, the writer makes the reader sympathise with Tom and share his feelings towards Laurence.

To what extent do you agree or disagree with this statement?

In your response you could:

- write about your own impressions of the half-brothers and their relationship
- comment on how the writer has created these impressions
- support your response with references to the text.

(20 marks)

Exam Practice — Paper 1, Reading 3

Spend about 15 minutes reading the source material below and the four questions on pages 55–56.

This extract is from a short story, *The Doll's House* by Katherine Mansfield, first published in 1921. The Burnell sisters have been given a new doll's house.

The Burnell children could hardly walk to school fast enough the next morning. They burned to tell everybody, to describe, to – well – to boast about their doll's house before the school-bell rang.

5 'I'm to tell,' said Isabel, 'because I'm the eldest. And you two can join in after. But I'm to tell first.'

There was nothing to answer. Isabel was bossy, but she was always right, and Lottie and Kezia knew too well the powers that went with being eldest. They brushed through the thick buttercups at the road edge and said nothing.

'And I'm to choose who's to come and see it first. Mother said I might.'

10 For it had been arranged that while the doll's house stood in the courtyard they might ask the girls at school, two at a time, to come and look. Not to stay to tea, of course, or to come traipsing through the house. But just to stand quietly in the courtyard while Isabel pointed out the beauties, and Lottie and Kezia looked pleased …

15 But hurry as they might, by the time they had reached the tarred palings of the boys' playground the bell had begun to jangle. They only just had time to whip off their hats and fall into line before the roll was called. Never mind. Isabel tried to make up for it by looking very important and mysterious and by whispering behind her hand to the girls near her, 'Got something to tell you at playtime.'

20 Playtime came and Isabel was surrounded. The girls of her class nearly fought to put their arms round her, to walk away with her, to beam flatteringly, to be her special friend. She held quite a court under the huge pine trees at the side of the playground. Nudging, giggling together, the little girls pressed up close. And the only two who stayed outside the ring were the two who were always outside, the little Kelveys. They knew better than to come anywhere near the Burnells.

25 For the fact was, the school the Burnell children went to was not at all the kind of place their parents would have chosen if there had been any choice. But there was none. It was the only school for miles. And the consequence was all the children of the neighbourhood, the Judge's little girls, the doctor's daughters, the store-keeper's children, the milkman's, were forced to mix together. Not to speak of there being an equal number of rude, rough little boys as well. But the line had to be drawn somewhere. It was drawn at the Kelveys. Many of the children, including 30 the Burnells, were not allowed even to speak to them. They walked past the Kelveys with their heads in the air, and as they set the fashion in all matters of behaviour, the Kelveys were shunned by everybody. Even the teacher had a special voice for them, and a special smile for the other children when Lil Kelvey came up to her desk with a bunch of dreadfully common-looking flowers.

35 They were the daughters of a spry, hardworking little washerwoman, who went about from house to house by the day. This was awful enough. But where was Mr Kelvey? Nobody knew for certain. But everybody said he was in prison. So they were the daughters of a washerwoman and a gaolbird. Very nice company for other people's children! And they looked it. Why Mrs Kelvey made them so conspicuous was hard to understand. The truth was they were dressed in 'bits' given 40 to her by the people for whom she worked. Lil, for instance, who was a stout, plain child, with big

freckles, came to school in a dress made from a green art-serge table-cloth of the Burnells', with red plush sleeves from the Logans' curtains. Her hat, perched on top of her high forehead, was a grown-up woman's hat, once the property of Miss Lecky, the postmistress. It was turned up at the back and trimmed with a large scarlet quill. What a little guy she looked! It was impossible not to laugh. And her little sister, our Else, wore a long white dress, rather like a nightgown, and a pair of little boy's boots. But whatever our Else wore she would have looked strange. She was a tiny wishbone of a child, with cropped hair and enormous solemn eyes – a little white owl. Nobody had ever seen her smile; she scarcely ever spoke. She went through life holding on to Lil, with a piece of Lil's skirt screwed up in her hand. Where Lil went, our Else followed. In the playground, on the road going to and from school, there was Lil marching in front and our Else holding on behind. Only when she wanted anything, or when she was out of breath, our Else gave Lil a tug, a twitch, and Lil stopped and turned round. The Kelveys never failed to understand each other.

Now they hovered at the edge; you couldn't stop them listening. When the little girls turned round and sneered, Lil, as usual, gave her silly, shamefaced smile, but our Else only looked.

And Isabel's voice, so very proud, went on telling.

Question 1

Re-read the first part of the source, from lines 1 to 8 (to '... said nothing.').

Tick (✓) one box for each question.

a) Why can the children hardly walk fast enough?

- They are late for school ☐
- They are arguing ☐
- They are so keen to get to school ☐

b) Why does Isabel think she should be first to tell people about the doll's house?

- She is the eldest ☐
- It is her doll's house ☐
- She is always right ☐

c) How do Lottie and Kezia respond to Isabel?

- They argue with her ☐
- They start to cry ☐
- They say nothing ☐

d) What do we learn about Isabel?

- She is bossy ☐
- She is quiet ☐
- She is kind to her sisters ☐

(4 marks)

Question 2

Look in detail at the following extract, from lines 9 to 21 of the source.

> 'And I'm to choose who's to come and see it first. Mother said I might.'
>
> For it had been arranged that while the doll's house stood in the courtyard they might ask the girls at school, two at a time, to come and look. Not to stay to tea, of course, or to come traipsing through the house. But just to stand quietly in the courtyard while Isabel pointed out the beauties, and Lottie and Kezia looked pleased ...
>
> But hurry as they might, by the time they had reached the tarred palings of the boys' playground the bell had begun to jangle. They only just had time to whip off their hats and fall into line before the roll was called. Never mind. Isabel tried to make up for it by looking very important and mysterious and by whispering behind her hand to the girls near her, 'Got something to tell you at playtime.'
>
> Playtime came and Isabel was surrounded. The girls of her class nearly fought to put their arms round her, to walk away with her, to beam flatteringly, to be her special friend. She held quite a court under the huge pine trees at the side of the playground.

How does the writer use language here to describe the Burnell sisters, their response to the doll's house and the other girls' reactions to them?

You could include the writer's choice of:

- words and phrases
- language features and techniques
- sentence forms.

(8 marks)

Question 3

You now need to think about the whole of the source.

The text is from a short story.

How has the writer structured the text to create a sense of pecking order among the children and their families?

You could write about:

- how differences between the children and families are described
- how and why the writer shifts the focus to the Kelveys
- the writer's use of any other structural features, such as changes in mood, tone or perspective. (8 marks)

Question 4

Focus this part of your answer on the second part of the source, from line 19 ('Playtime came ...') to the end.

It could be said that the writer here exposes the cruelty both of the children and of the society they live in.

To what extent do you agree or disagree with this statement?

In your response you could:

- write about your own impressions of the actions and attitudes depicted in the story
- comment on how the writer has created these impressions
- support your response with references to the text.

(20 marks)

Exam Practice — Paper 1, Reading 4

Spend about 15 minutes reading the source material below and the four questions on pages 58–59.

This extract is the opening of a novel, *The History of Mr Polly* by H.G. Wells, first published in 1910.

'Hole!' said Mr Polly, and then for a change, and with greatly increased emphasis: 'Ole!' He paused, and then broke out with one of his private and peculiar idioms. 'Oh! Beastly Silly Wheeze of a Hole!' He was sitting on a stile between two threadbare looking fields, and suffering acutely from indigestion.

He suffered from indigestion now nearly every afternoon in his life, but as he lacked introspection he projected the associated discomfort upon the world. Every afternoon he discovered afresh that life as a whole and every aspect of life that presented itself was 'beastly'. And this afternoon, lured by the delusive blueness of a sky that was blue because the wind was in the east, he had come out in the hope of snatching something of the joyousness of spring. The mysterious alchemy of mind and body refused, however, to permit any joyousness whatever in the spring.

He had had a little difficulty in finding his cap before he came out. He wanted his cap – the new golf cap – and Mrs Polly must needs fish out his old soft brown felt hat. ''Ere's your 'at,' she said in a tone of insincere encouragement.

He had been rooting among the piled newspapers under the kitchen dresser, and had turned quite hopefully and taken the thing. He put it on. But it didn't feel right. Nothing felt right. He put a trembling hand upon the crown of the thing and pressed it on his head, and tried it askew to the right and then askew to the left.

Then the full sense of the indignity offered him came home to him. The hat masked the upper sinister quarter[1] of his face, and he spoke with a wrathful eye regarding his wife from under the brim. In a voice thick with fury he said: 'I s'pose you'd like me to wear that silly Mud Pie for ever, eh? I tell you I won't. I'm sick of it. I'm pretty near sick of everything, comes to that … Hat!'

He clutched it with quivering fingers. 'Hat!' he repeated. Then he flung it to the ground, and kicked it with extraordinary fury across the kitchen. It flew up against the door and dropped to the ground with its ribbon band half off.

'Shan't go out!' he said, and sticking his hands into his jacket pockets discovered the missing cap in the right one.

There was nothing for it but to go straight upstairs without a word, and out, slamming the shop door hard.

'Beauty!' said Mrs Polly at last to a tremendous silence, picking up and dusting the rejected headdress. 'Tantrums,' she added. 'I 'aven't patience.' And moving with the slow reluctance of a deeply offended woman, she began to pile together the simple apparatus of their recent meal, for transportation to the scullery sink.

The repast she had prepared for him did not seem to her to justify his ingratitude. There had been the cold pork from Sunday and some nice cold potatoes, and Rashdall's Mixed Pickles, of which he was inordinately fond. He had eaten three gherkins, two onions, a small cauliflower head and several capers with every appearance of appetite, and indeed with avidity; and then there had been cold suet pudding to follow, with treacle, and then a nice bit of cheese. It was the pale, hard sort of cheese he liked; red cheese he declared was indigestible. He had also had three

40 big slices of greyish baker's bread, and had drunk the best part of the jugful of beer ... But there seems to be no pleasing some people.

'Tantrums!' said Mrs Polly at the sink, struggling with the mustard on his plate and expressing the only solution of the problem that occurred to her.

45 And Mr Polly sat on the stile and hated the whole scheme of life – which was at once excessive and inadequate as a solution. He hated Foxbourne, he hated Foxbourne High Street, he hated his shop and his wife and his neighbours – every blessed neighbour – and with indescribable bitterness he hated himself.

'Why did I ever get in this silly Hole?' he said. 'Why did I ever?'

[1] In this context, the left.

Question 1

Re-read the first part of the source, from lines 1 to 11 (to '... in the spring.').

Tick (✓) one box for each question.

a) Where is Mr Polly sitting?

　In a hole　☐

　On a stile　☐

　In a field　☐

b) What ailment does Mr Polly suffer from?

　Headaches　☐

　Indigestion　☐

　Asthma　☐

c) How does Mr Polly respond to his discomfort?

　Patiently　☐

　He tries to keep moving　☐

　He blames the world　☐

d) Why has Mr Polly left the house?

　To try to enjoy the spring　☐

　For healthy exercise　☐

　To do some thinking　☐

(4 marks)

Question 2

Look in detail at the following extract, from lines 12 to 22 of the source.

> He had had a little difficulty in finding his cap before he came out. He wanted his cap – the new golf cap – and Mrs Polly must needs fish out his old soft brown felt hat. ''Ere's your 'at,' she said in a tone of insincere encouragement.
>
> He had been rooting among the piled newspapers under the kitchen dresser, and had turned quite hopefully and taken the thing. He put it on. But it didn't feel right. Nothing felt right. He put a trembling hand upon the crown of the thing and pressed it on his head, and tried it askew to the right and then askew to the left.
>
> Then the full sense of the indignity offered him came home to him. The hat masked the upper sinister quarter of his face, and he spoke with a wrathful eye regarding his wife from under the brim. In a voice thick with fury he said: 'I s'pose you'd like me to wear that silly Mud Pie for ever, eh? I tell you I won't. I'm sick of it. I'm pretty near sick of everything, comes to that… Hat!'

How does the writer use language here to convey Mr Polly's feelings and mood?

You could include the writer's choice of:

- words and phrases
- language features and techniques
- sentence forms.

(8 marks)

Question 3

You now need to think about the whole of the source.

The text is the opening of a novel.

How has the writer structured the text to create a sense of Mr Polly's character and life?

You could write about:

- what the writer focuses your attention on at the beginning of this extract
- how the writer uses structure to create effects
- the writer's use of any other structural features, such as changes in mood, tone or perspective.

(8 marks)

Question 4

Focus this part of your answer on the second part of the source, from line 23 ('He clutched it ...') to the end.

It could be said that here the writer humorously conveys the feeling that Mr Jolly is dissatisfied with everyday life.

To what extent do you agree or disagree with this statement?

In your response you could:

- write about your own impressions of Mr Polly, his life and his feelings
- comment on how the writer has created these impressions
- support your response with references to the text.

(20 marks)

Exam Practice — Paper 2 Reading 1

Spend about 15 minutes reading the two sources on pages 60–61 and the four questions on page 62.

Source A

This is a newspaper article by Marianne Ripley.

While I care for the carers, who cares about me?

Marianne Ripley on the trials and tribulations of the single working mother.

'I know I'm better off than most …'; 'I'm very lucky really …'. How many times do we single mothers hear such phrases dropping from our lips? But why apologise for telling the truth? It is difficult bringing up children on your own. It's difficult juggling work and home life. And I never imagined just how difficult it would be to find decent childcare.

My two are five and three. One's just started school and the other is at home. Out in the country where we live there are no suitable nurseries that can take her and I can't give up work. I don't have the luxury of the on-tap doting grandparents that so many working parents seem to benefit from. So I have to pay someone to look after Maisie every day and Lottie for a couple of hours after school and in the holidays.

Someone in the village recommended 'a very nice lady' who had 'loads of experience' and had nurtured generations of village children. She was a little elderly but very smiley and welcoming. Her house was spotless and she was up-to-date with all the latest rules and regulations from basic hygiene to child protection. She couldn't collect Lottie from school – but 'if I didn't object' she was sure her daughter-in-law Rowena would oblige, as she'd be picking up her own two anyway. What's more, Mrs Snedwell (I couldn't bring myself to call her by her first name – she seemed to demand respect) had no other 'kiddywinkies' at the moment, so she'd be happy to look after Maisie in my house if that suited.

You bet it did. And the next six months were blissful. The girls loved Mrs Snedwell. She played with them, read to them, kept them entertained with rather far-fetched stories of life in the olden days, and even did a spot of cleaning now and again ('Ooh, you don't need to pay me extra, dear. I enjoy it!').

But then everything changed. Sadly, Mrs Snedwell had a stroke. Rowena brought the news. As polite as her mother-in-law, she couldn't stop apologising for the inconvenience but was sure I'd understand. Of course I did. Mrs Snedwell thankfully recovered but wasn't up to child-minding anymore. I put a card in the post office window. Rowena 'put the feelers out'. I asked at the school. The best anyone could come up with was an unemployed twenty-year-old girl from the next village. Still, she had a qualification in nursery nursing and she'd had her checks done …

So I gave her a go. It didn't take long before I found out why she couldn't find a job. Unpunctual, slovenly, constantly in tears about something or other (usually a boyfriend), she showed little interest in the children. What's more, whenever I got home from work I had to sit and listen while she poured her heart out. Then I had to give her a lift back home. Then, when I got back, I had to clear up the mess she'd left behind. I had to let her go.

Her replacement was completely different. A rather sophisticated, terribly chic young woman from the south of France. She was pretty. She was personable. She charmed the children. However, if the previous childminder was an emotional wreck, this one was a total disaster area. Insecurities, romantic entanglements, home-sickness. She had the lot. And, after six weeks, she went.

And so it went on. Childminders, au pairs, nannies, babysitters, drifting in and out of our lives, some staying for a few months and some for a couple of days. And almost every one of them more emotionally demanding and time consuming than the children they were paid to look after. And I know I'm very lucky … There I go again. I'm lucky to have two delightful daughters. I'm lucky to have a decent job and a nice home. And I was lucky to have Mrs Snedwell, but I'd feel so much luckier if I could find someone else who might take care of my children without expecting me to take care of them.

Source B

This extract is from *The Life of Charlotte Brontë* by Elizabeth Gaskell, a biography first published in 1857. Here Mrs Gaskell describes the family's household in Haworth, Yorkshire, after the deaths of Charlotte's mother and two oldest sisters.

For the reason just stated, the little girls were sent home in the autumn of 1825, when Charlotte was little more than nine years old.

About this time, an elderly woman of the village came to live as servant at the parsonage. She remained there, as a member of the household, for thirty years; and from the length of her faithful service, and the attachment and respect which she inspired, is deserving of mention. Tabby was a thorough specimen of a Yorkshire woman of her class, in dialect, in appearance, and in character. She abounded in strong practical sense and shrewdness. Her words were far from flattery; but she would spare no deeds in the cause of those whom she kindly regarded. She ruled the children pretty sharply; and yet never grudged a little extra trouble to provide them with such small treats as came within her power. In return, she claimed to be looked upon as a humble friend; and, many years later, Miss Brontë told me that she found it somewhat difficult to manage, as Tabby expected to be informed of all the family concerns, and yet had grown so deaf that what was repeated to her became known to whoever might be in or about the house. To obviate this publication of what it might be desirable to keep secret, Miss Brontë used to take her out for a walk on the solitary moors; where, when both were seated on a tuft of heather, in some high lonely place, she could acquaint the old woman, at leisure, with all that she wanted to hear.

Tabby had lived in Haworth in the days when the pack-horses went through once a week, with their tinkling bells and gay worsted[1] adornment, carrying the produce of the country from Keighley over the hills to Colne and Burnley. What is more, she had known the 'bottom', or valley, in those primitive days when the fairies frequented the margin of the 'beck'[2] on moonlight nights, and had known folk who had seen them. But that was when there were no mills in the valleys; and when all the wool-spinning was done by hand in the farm-houses round. 'It wur the factories as had driven 'em away,' she said. No doubt she had many a tale to tell of by-gone days of the country-side; old ways of living, former inhabitants, decayed gentry, who had melted away, and whose places knew them no more; family tragedies, and dark superstitious dooms; and in telling these things, without the least consciousness that there might ever be anything requiring to be softened down, would give at full length the bare and simple details.

Miss Branwell[3] instructed the children at regular hours in all she could teach, making her bed-chamber into their schoolroom. Their father was in the habit of relating to them any public news in which he felt an interest; and from the opinions of his strong and independent mind they would gather much food for thought; but I do not know whether he gave them any direct instruction. Charlotte's deep thoughtful spirit appears to have felt almost painfully the tender responsibility which rested upon her with reference to her remaining sisters. She was only eighteen months older than Emily; but Emily and Anne were simply companions and playmates, while Charlotte was motherly friend and guardian to both; and this loving assumption of duties beyond her years, made her feel considerably older than she really was.

Patrick Branwell, their only brother, was a boy of remarkable promise, and, in some ways, of extraordinary precocity of talent. Mr Brontë's friends advised him to send his son to school; but, remembering both the strength of will of his own youth and his mode of employing it, he believed that Patrick was better at home, and that he himself could teach him well, as he had taught others before. So Patrick, or as his family called him – Branwell, remained at Haworth, working hard for some hours a day with his father; but, when the time of the latter was taken up with his parochial duties, the boy was thrown into chance companionship with the lads of the village – for youth will to youth, and boys will to boys.

[1] worsted – cloth made from fine wool
[2] beck – Yorkshire name for a brook or stream
[3] Miss Branwell – Charlotte's aunt, the sister of the Brontës' mother

Question 1

Re-read the first part of Source A, from lines 1 to 9 (to '... and in the holidays').

Choose four statements below which are true. Tick or shade in the boxes of the ones that you think are true.

a) The writer is a single mother. ☐
b) The writer lives in the city. ☐
c) The writer has three children. ☐
d) The writer works. ☐
e) One of the children is at school. ☐
f) The children's grandparents look after them. ☐
g) Lottie does not need childcare. ☐
h) The writer thinks being a single mother is hard. ☐

(4 marks)

Question 2

You need to refer to Source A and Source B for this question.

The Brontë children and the Ripley children are both looked after by carers.

What can you infer about the differences between how the two sets of children are cared for?

(8 marks)

Question 3

You now need to refer only to Source B, lines 16–25 (from 'Tabby had lived ...' to '... simple details.').

How does the writer use language to describe Tabby?   (12 marks)

Question 4

For this question you need to refer to the whole of Source A together with the whole of Source B.

Compare how the writers convey their different feelings and perspectives about people who look after the children they are writing about.

In your answer you could:

- compare the different attitudes shown
- comment on the methods the writers use to convey these attitudes
- support your response with references to both texts.

(16 marks)

Exam Practice — Paper 2 Reading 2

Spend about 15 minutes reading the two sources on pages 63–64 and the four questions on page 65.

Source A

This extract is from a letter by Charles Dickens, 'Crime and Education', published in *The Daily News* on 4 February 1846. Making the link between lack of education and crime, he describes a visit to a 'Ragged School', a charitable school set up by the church to teach children too poor to be able to pay for school.

For the instruction, and as a first step in the reformation, of such unhappy beings, the Ragged Schools were founded. I was first attracted to the subject, and indeed was first made conscious of their existence, about two years ago, or more, by seeing an advertisement in the papers dated from West Street, Saffron Hill, stating 'That a room had been opened and supported in that wretched neighbourhood for upwards of twelve months, where religious instruction had been imparted to the poor', and explaining in a few words what was meant by Ragged Schools as a generic term, including, then, four or five similar places of instruction. I wrote to the masters of this particular school to make some further inquiries, and went myself soon afterwards.

It was a hot summer night; and the air of Field Lane and Saffron Hill was not improved by such weather, nor were the people in those streets very sober or honest company. Being unacquainted with the exact locality of the school, I was fain to make some inquiries about it. These were very jocosely received in general; but everybody knew where it was, and gave the right direction to it. The prevailing idea among the loungers (the greater part of them the very sweepings of the streets and station houses) seemed to be, that the teachers were quixotic[1], and the school upon the whole 'a lark'. But there was certainly a kind of rough respect for the intention, and (as I have said) nobody denied the school or its whereabouts, or refused assistance in directing to it.

It consisted at that time of either two or three – I forget which – miserable rooms, upstairs in a miserable house. In the best of these, the pupils in the female school were being taught to read and write; and though there were the number, many wretched creatures steeped in degradation to the lips, they were tolerably quiet, and listened with apparent earnestness and patience to their instructors.

The appearance of this room was sad and melancholy, of course – how could it be otherwise! – but, on the whole, encouraging.

The close, low chamber at the back, in which the boys were crowded, was so foul and stifling as to be, at first, almost insupportable. But its moral aspect was so far worse than its physical, that this was soon forgotten. Huddled together on a bench about the room, and shown out by some flaring candles stuck against the walls, were a crowd of boys, varying from mere infants to young men; sellers of fruit, herbs, lucifer-matches, flints; sleepers under the dry arches of bridges; young thieves and beggars – with nothing natural to youth about them: with nothing frank, ingenuous, or pleasant in their faces; low-browed, vicious, cunning, wicked; abandoned of all help but this; speeding downward to destruction; and UNUTTERABLY IGNORANT.

I have no desire to praise the system pursued in the Ragged Schools; which is necessarily very imperfect, if indeed there be one.

This was the Class I saw at the Ragged School. They could not be trusted with books; they could only be instructed orally; they were difficult of reduction to anything like attention, obedience, or decent behaviour; their benighted ignorance in reference to the Deity, or to any social duty (how could they guess at any social duty, being so discarded by all social teachers but the gaoler and the hangman!) was terrible to see. Yet, even here, and among these, something had been done already.

The Ragged School was of recent date and very poor; but it had inculcated some association with the name of the Almighty, which was not an oath, and had taught them to look forward in a hymn (they sang it) to another life, which would correct the miseries and woes of this.

[1] enthusiastic and idealistic but impractical

Source B

This is an article from a parents' website by Andrew Stringer.

NOW HEALTH AND SAFETY REALLY HAVE GONE MAD!

It's become such a cliché, hasn't it? Health and Safety gone mad! Yes, I appreciate there is a need for some rules and regulations around health and safety. We need to be healthy. We need to be safe. And sometimes we need a little help with that. But after what I've experienced in the last few weeks, I'm beginning to think health and safety really have gone mad.

First, I got drawn into the whole 'Healthy Schools' business. No, it's not something made up by soap opera scriptwriters or reactionary newspaper columnists, it's really happening in schools all over the country. Including my daughter's school. Phoebe is seven. She goes to the local state primary, a lovely school, full of bright, happy children and caring teachers, where she was very happy … Until last Friday.

She came home in tears because a dinner lady had 'stolen her sweets'! This ogress is apparently paid to stand at the entrance to the school dining room and inspect the children's lunch boxes as they enter. If there's anything in there that appears on a list of forbidden foods – sweets, biscuits, sausage rolls, fizzy drinks – she confiscates it. And it seems the headteacher is right behind her; the governors are right behind her; and the government is right behind them. It's called 'The Healthy Schools Initiative' or some such nonsense.

Well, I'm sorry. But we're her parents. We are responsible for seeing that she's fit and healthy. We make sure she has a balanced diet. We also happen to believe that the occasional treat is not going to ruin her health. What our daughter eats should be down to us, not the Health Fascists.

And if that's not enough, have you heard about the headteacher who's banned footballs in the playground? No, it's not a joke. The headteacher of a primary school just down the road from us has banned children from playing football in the playground. Why? Because the balls might 'injure the children'. And he's not the only one.

So, on the one hand, the government is lecturing us about doing more sport to keep fit, while on the other hand, their minions, like this crazed headteacher (who obviously hasn't got any real work to do), ban our children from playing the national game.

And all this is happening at a time when, according to a recent study from Sheffield University, 17% of our young people leave school 'functionally illiterate'. That's after at least eleven years of so-called education! Perhaps it's time our teachers, headteachers, school governors and the government started to focus on teaching the children how to read and write rather than obsessing about 'health and safety'.

Do health and safety matter? Of course they do. But let's use a little common sense, put more trust in parents' ability to make their own decisions, and let schools do what they were set up to do. In other words, you stick to your job and let us parents do ours.

Question 1

Re-read the first part of Source A, from lines 1 to 9 (to '... honest company.').

Choose **four** statements below which are true. Tick or shade in the boxes of the ones that you think are true.

a) The school had only just opened when Dickens visited it. ☐

b) Dickens learned about the Ragged Schools from a newspaper. ☐

c) The purpose of the school was to give religious instruction to the poor. ☐

d) Dickens helped to set up the school. ☐

e) The advertisement in the paper explained what Ragged Schools were. ☐

f) Dickens was not interested in the Ragged Schools. ☐

g) The school was in the Saffron Hill area. ☐

h) The people he met in the streets were honest. ☐ (4 marks)

Question 2

You need to refer to Source A and Source B for this question.

The writers in Source A and Source B both describe schools.

What can you infer about the differences between the two schools? (8 marks)

Question 3

You now need to refer only to Source B, lines 1 to 29 (to '... not the Health Fascists').

How does the writer use language to express his feelings about his daughter's experience? (12 marks)

Question 4

For this question you need to refer to the whole of Source A together with the whole of Source B.

Compare how the writers convey attitudes to education.

In your answer you could:

- compare the different attitudes shown
- comment on the methods the writers use to convey these attitudes
- support your response with references to both texts. (16 marks)

Exam Practice

Paper 2 Reading 3

Spend about 15 minutes reading the two sources on pages 66–67 and the four questions on page 68.

Source A

This is an article written by John Edwards for a local newspaper.

Westerley Needs You!

And it certainly needs its local post office, according to villager John Edwards.

Alice Morris is eighty-three. She's lived in Little Billington all her life. I met her last week outside the village post office in Westerley.

5 Alice was waiting for a taxi to take her five miles back to her own village. It had dropped her off just half an hour earlier to withdraw some money, pay a few bills and buy 'a couple of bits and pieces' to keep her going until the weekend. There's no post office in Little Billington since it was closed three years ago. This is the nearest one for Alice and, as she's got no car, there's no bus service and, in her own words, she's 'a bit shaky on my pins', a taxi is the only way she can get around. It costs her almost twenty pounds a time. A lot of money for a pensioner.

10 I've got bad news for Alice and all the other pensioners in the villages and hamlets surrounding Westerley. If the Post Office (by which I mean the massive profit-making company that runs the service across the UK, not the little shop in the village) has its way, she'll have to travel a lot further and spend a lot more on taxis in the future. It's been announced that Westerley Post Office could close by the end of the year. According to the couple who manage it, there just isn't enough business to keep the post office

15 going. In theory, Westerley serves a population of over ten thousand people. However, a lot of things we used to use the post office for can be done online now, so fewer people visit their post office regularly. And, of course, fewer letters are being sent, though many post offices have seen an increase in parcels being sent and collected.

In view of all this, closure seems like a sensible option, but it misses the point entirely. It's not just about
20 profitability. The post office is a lifeline for people like Alice. Not just pensioners, many of whom still go to the post office to draw out cash, but mothers with young children, people with mobility problems and those who can't afford to get taxis into the nearest town (ten miles away) just to send someone a birthday present or withdraw a few pounds from their bank.

And it's not just post office services people are worried about. According to Sid and Else, who run the
25 post office and shop, if the post office goes, the shop might have to go too. At the moment, Sid gets in the region of £12,000 a year as sub-postmaster, a salary which, though not massive, enables the couple to keep the shop going. Profits from the shop, they say, would not justify opening every weekday from nine to five-thirty as they do now. They might manage a few days a week. Or they might shut up shop for good.

It's a depressingly familiar story of rural decline. The village bobby, the village school, the bus service, all
30 gone in so many places. Over 4000 local post offices have closed since 1999 and there are plans for many more to go. But there are rays of hope. Here and there across the country, villagers are beginning to fight back. In Lincolnshire, a local family has saved their post office by opening a tea room. In Essex, two brothers have combined the post office with a pharmacy. Elsewhere, villagers have rallied round to buy local shops and run them as community enterprises in a bid to keep local services going.

35 Whether it's diversification or community-takeover, Westerly too needs to do something to save its post office. Remember that word 'could'. The post office hasn't closed yet. 'Could' doesn't mean 'will'. It's up to all of us to fight its closure and if we can't persuade the powers-that-be from the Post Office that it's worth keeping open, we need to prove them wrong by taking action to save our post office and our community.

Source B

This extract is from a letter to *The Scotsman* newspaper, published in 1873. In it, the writer, who signs himself 'NOT A SUB-POSTMASTER', describes the work of the people who run local post offices (sub-postmasters) and complains that their work is unappreciated and undervalued.

Take for example, the work of a sub-office in a district where there is about 1000 of a population, making up and receiving say sixteen or eighteen bags a-day, with money-orders and telegraph messages averaging eight or ten a-day. Consider the amount of writing those money-orders and telegraph messages entail, the numerous entries to be made in order to account for cash received and cash paid. Also consider the work necessitated by the stamping and arranging of letters, the sale of stamps, and the attendance required by the public in supplying them with information on all matters connected with the department. This work is quite sufficient to occupy the whole time of one individual, and it could be accomplished by him if nature had endowed him with a constitution that would go on working for ever without relaxation. For, granting there may be only one telegraph message, money-order, or savings bank transaction a day, in place of eight or eighteen, the acting postmaster must be at his post, to wait for the call that may be made for him at anytime. His time belongs to that hard task-master the public, from seven in the morning until eight at night, and if in a country office, the bags are to be made up after that. For this work, filling up the entire time of an educated man or woman, the sub-postmaster may consider himself extremely fortunate if he receives 12 s . 6 d per week! It must be patent to all that no sub-postmaster can live on the salary he receives for his work from the Post Office; he must have some other source of income. The salaries of all sub-postmasters are based on the assumption that their whole time is not occupied; whereas it is impossible for one individual to do this work, at least to do it continuously.

Mr Monsell stated in Parliament recently that the Post Office authorities found no difficulty in getting sub-postmasters to take office. This statement must be received with some limitation, as until installed in office they can have no idea what is expected of them, while those who are in office have their mouths in a measure shut.

If the office of sub-postmaster was one highly esteemed we might suppose that the honour of the position compensated for the lack of emoluments; but such is not the case. The village postmaster is always opening somebody's letter, and stealing somebody's postage stamps.

He gets scant courtesy from the public, and should he offend some village somebody in discharging his duty or observing rules made by the service, he gets no support from his superiors. Let any postmaster refuse, whether courteously or not, to open a sealed letter-bag and put in some local or city bigwig's late letter, a report is at once sent to the Secretary complaining of the incivility of the sub-postmaster.

Fete-days or fast-days are alike to the sub-postmaster. The shopkeeper can close his shop and take a holiday, but the office work must go on as usual and should health totally fail, even then no relief is given him.

The sub-postmaster may in reality die at his post so far as the service cares, for, unless he can pay for a substitute he can get no relief. As telegraphists and sub-postmasters, unlike poets, are trained and made, not born, even this arrangement may be impossible; yet after all the sub-postmaster is 'a man and a brother'.

These are plain facts; hundreds of postmasters can, if they choose, vouch for their accuracy. They begin to see that the matter lies very much in their own hands. It rests with themselves to show that Mr Monsell's statement is not a correct one, that they are overworked and underpaid, and that they are prepared to use every lawful means to have their wrongs redressed …

The claims of such an important class of labourers ought to find some advocates from the general public.

Question 1

Re-read the first part of Source A, from lines 1 to 9 (to 'A lot of money for a pensioner.').

Choose **four** statements below which are true. Tick or shade in the boxes of the ones that you think are true.

a) Alice Morris lives in Westerley. ☐

b) There are regular buses from Little Billington. ☐

c) Alice Morris is eighty-three. ☐

d) It is five miles from Little Billington to Westerley. ☐

e) Alice walks from her home to the post office. ☐

f) Westerley Post Office has been closed. ☐

g) Alice uses the post office to withdraw money. ☐

h) Alice is dependent on taxis. ☐

(4 marks)

Question 2

You need to refer to Source A and Source B for this question.

The writers of Source A and Source B both describe post offices.

What can you infer about the differences between the two post offices? (8 marks)

Question 3

You now need to refer only to Source B, lines 22 ('If the office ...') to 33 ('... "a man and a brother".').

How does the writer use language to express his feelings about how sub-postmasters are treated? (12 marks)

Question 4

For this question you need to refer to the whole of Source A together with the whole of Source B.

Compare how the writers convey their different feelings and perspectives on post offices.

In your answer you could:

- compare the different attitudes shown
- comment on the methods the writers use to convey their perspectives
- support your response with references to both texts. (16 marks)

Exam Practice — Paper 2 Reading 4

Spend about 15 minutes reading the two sources on pages 69–71 and the four questions on pages 71–72.

Source A

This extract is from *Mrs Beeton's Book of Household Management* by Isabella Beeton, published in 1861. In this section, Mrs Beeton gives advice about holding an evening party or ball.

AS THE LADIES AND GENTLEMEN ARRIVE, each should be shown to a room exclusively provided for their reception; and in that set apart for the ladies, attendants should be in waiting to assist in uncloaking, and helping to arrange the hair and toilet of those who require it. It will be found convenient, in those cases where the number of guests is large, to provide numbered tickets, so that they
5 can be attached to the cloaks and shawls of each lady, a duplicate of which should be handed to the guest. Coffee is sometimes provided in this, or an ante-room, for those who would like to partake of it.

AS THE VISITORS ARE ANNOUNCED BY THE SERVANT, it is not necessary for the lady of the house to advance each time towards the door, but merely to rise from her seat to receive their courtesies and congratulations. If, indeed, the hostess wishes to show particular favour to some peculiarly honoured
10 guests, she may introduce them to others, whose acquaintance she may imagine will be especially suitable and agreeable. It is very often the practice of the master of the house to introduce one gentleman to another, but occasionally the lady performs this office; when it will, of course, be polite for the persons thus introduced to take their seats together for the time being.

A SEPARATE ROOM OR CONVENIENT BUFFET should be appropriated for refreshments, and to
15 which the dancers may retire; and cakes and biscuits, with wine negus, lemonade, and ices, handed round. A supper is also mostly provided at the private parties of the middle classes; and this requires, on the part of the hostess, a great deal of attention and supervision. It usually takes place between the first and second parts of the programme of the dances, of which there should be several prettily written or printed copies distributed about the ball-room.

20 *In private parties*, a lady is not to refuse the invitation of a gentleman to dance, unless she be previously engaged. The hostess must be supposed to have asked to her house only those persons whom she knows to be perfectly respectable and of unblemished character, as well as pretty equal in position; and thus, to decline the offer of any gentleman present, would be a tacit reflection on the master and mistress of the house. It may be mentioned here, more especially for the young who will read this
25 book, that introductions at balls or evening parties, cease with the occasion that calls them forth, no introduction, at these times, giving a gentleman a right to address, afterwards, a lady. She is, consequently, free, next morning, to pass her partner at a ball of the previous evening without the slightest recognition.

THE BALL IS GENERALLY OPENED, that is, the first place in the first quadrille is occupied, by the
30 lady of the house. When anything prevents this, the host will usually lead off the dance with the lady who is either the highest in rank, or the greatest stranger. It will be well for the hostess, even if she be very partial to the amusement, and a graceful dancer, not to participate in it to any great extent, lest her lady guests should have occasion to complain of her monopoly of the gentlemen, and other causes of neglect. A few dances will suffice to show her interest in the entertainment, without unduly trenching on the
35 attention due to her guests. In all its parts a ball should be perfect,—

'The music, and the banquet, and the wine;
The garlands, the rose-odours, and the flowers.'

The hostess or host, during the progress of a ball, will courteously accost and chat with their friends, and take care that the ladies are furnished with seats, and that those who wish to dance are provided
40 with partners. A gentle hint from the hostess, conveyed in a quiet ladylike

manner, that certain ladies have remained unengaged during several dances, is sure not to be neglected by any gentleman. Thus will be studied the comfort and enjoyment of the guests, and no lady, in leaving the house, will be able to feel the chagrin and disappointment of not having been invited to 'stand up' in a dance during the whole of the evening.

45 WHEN ANY OF THE CARRIAGES OF THE GUESTS ARE ANNOUNCED, or the time for their departure arrived, they should make a slight intimation to the hostess, without, however, exciting any observation, that they are about to depart. If this cannot be done, however, without creating too much bustle, it will be better for the visitors to retire quietly without taking their leave. During the course of the week, the hostess will expect to receive from every guest a call, where it is possible, or cards expressing
50 the gratification experienced from her entertainment. This attention is due to every lady for the pains and trouble she has been at, and tends to promote social, kindly feelings.

Source B

This is a magazine article aimed at parents of teenagers.

School Proms: Love them or hate them, they're here to stay

Our tips on how to cope

Before the year 2000, school proms were virtually unheard of in the UK. Now nearly 90% of secondary schools hold them and an increasing number of primary schools are joining in the fun. The average cost of a prom to a girl's parents has been estimated as anything between £200 and a staggering £500 plus.
5 And don't think you won't have to worry about cost if you've got boys. They may not spend as much on their clothes, hair or spray tans as the girls, but they're catching up fast.

Whether driven by the Americanisation of our society or hard-nosed commercial interests exploiting the 'me generation' and its need to show off, we have to accept it. The prom is part of British life now. So we'd better learn to love it – or at least learn how to cope with it.

10 Nobody wants their child to be the one who stands out like a sore thumb, so here are some basics to help you get to grips with what's required and tips on how to avoid bankrupting your family.

Getting Ready

Forget 'don't judge a book by its cover' and 'looks don't matter'. How you look is The Most Important Thing about the school prom. Hair, make-up and, most importantly, The Dress have to be perfect. And
15 perfection takes planning – and money. Some parents indulge their offspring with high couture fashion, jewellery and visits to expensive beauty salons. The cost can run into hundreds or even thousands if you're not careful.

Our tip – this is the one area where you might find it very hard to skimp. You can't dress your daughter in charity shop clothes, unless you're lucky enough to have been blessed with an eccentric, rebellious eco
20 warrior. Mind you, it's well worth trying to appeal to her concerns about the planet (it's very on trend to care). Failing that, hiring might be an option. If you feel you have to buy, remember it's not always the most expensive outfits that make the biggest impression. And as for make-up and hair, you might be able to get a good deal for a group session for your daughter and her friends – not only cheaper but a lot more fun.

Getting There

25 Stretch limousines, Cinderella carriages, milk floats … we've all seen them and we've all wondered why they bother. The rest of the school is not going to be lined up waving flags as if your progeny were Will and Kate turning up for a royal wedding. They'll either be in transit themselves or already inside the venue.

Our tip – forget it. Persuade them it's a complete waste of money. Less spent on transport means more to spend on clothes. If they don't want to get the bus (and they won't in all that finery) offer them a lift. You could even go mad and pay for a taxi. But absolutely no sports cars, no tanks and no helicopters.

Being There

'There' could be anywhere from the school gym to a luxury country house hotel. If your school's any good, whoever's responsible for planning the prom will have taken into account what parents can reasonably expect to pay and, hopefully, have consulted you. Whatever the cost, though, one thing is certain. Once they've gone inside, it's not your problem. Relax. There'll be a strict no alcohol rule (unless they're over 18), illegal drugs will definitely be banned and you can rest assured that there'll be no fighting. School staff and staff from the venue will ensure that this will be one of the safest nights out your child will ever have – much less to worry about than at that party the neighbours' kids had when they were on holiday. The funny thing is that, although it might be safer than a hundredth birthday party in an old folks' home, they'll almost certainly remember their school prom as one of the best nights they've ever had in their lives.

Final Tip

It's going to cost you, but it needn't cost you the earth. Our top tip is to involve the young people in the financial planning. You're not the Clooneys and it's time your children realised it. Also, if the prom has any symbolic value, it's as a rite of passage into the adult world. Contrary to popular stereotypes, teenagers are not all feckless, selfish brats. They can and do take responsibility. So don't set them a bad example by going into debt for them. Tell them what your budget is and stick to it. If they want to spend more, suggest they contribute some of their pocket money or part-time earnings. And let them make informed choices about what to spend the money on. But, above all, don't lose sight of the fact that it's not about showing off – it's about fun, friendship and creating happy memories.

Question 1

Re-read the first part of Source A, from lines 1 to 6 (to '... partake of it.').

Choose **four** statements below which are true. Tick or shade in the boxes of the ones that you think are true.

a) On arrival, guests should be shown to a reception room. ☐

b) There should be people waiting to help ladies with their hair. ☐

c) Men have to wait on the step until the ladies are ready. ☐

d) Guests are asked to show their invitations when they arrive. ☐

e) Numbered tickets can be provided to help identify cloaks and shawls. ☐

f) Guests should keep their hats and coats with them at all times. ☐

g) Sometimes coffee is provided on arrival. ☐

h) Guests should be given a glass of wine when they arrive. ☐

(4 marks)

Question 2

You need to refer to Source A and Source B for this question.

Source A and Source B are both about different types of party.

What can you infer about the differences between the two types of party? (8 marks)

Question 3

You now need to refer only to Source B, lines 13 ('Forget "don't judge a book..."') to 23 ('... more fun.').

How does the writer use language to give advice to parents about the school prom? (12 marks)

Question 4

For this question, you need to refer to the whole of Source A together with the whole of Source B.

Compare how the writers convey their different feelings and perspectives about the kind of parties they describe.

In your answer you could:

- compare the different attitudes shown
- comment on the methods the writers use to convey their attitudes
- support your response with references to both texts. (16 marks)

Answers

Pages 4–5
Revise 1 Cheeses are often associated with particular regions. People in the UK eat huge amounts of cheese every year. … Both cheese and butter are made from milk. … Too much cheese might also be unhealthy.

Revise 2 The following answers are correct: a), c), d) and h).

Revise 3 b) Not about Mr Allworthy. **e)** Not stated in the text. **f)** Not about Mr Allworthy. **g)** Not stated in the text.

Extend Any four from: he was hearty/friendly; he was healthy; he was smart/dapper; he had a red face; he had thick/a shock of white hair; he was boisterous; he had a decided manner.

Pages 6–7
Revise 1 … But I don't like school. In fact, I hate it and I can't wait to leave. … I find the environment stifling. I find the lessons boring and irrelevant. I don't even like the depressing brutalist building. …

Revise 2 The following answers are correct: b), c), f) and h).

Revise 3 a) Not a plan but someone's opinion of the plans. **d)** Not stated in the text (we are only told that the current clerk is retiring). **e)** We are told that she is getting a new limousine. **g)** Not stated in the text.

Extend The following are correct: b), e), f) and g).

Pages 8–9
Revise 1 The following are correct: a), c) and d).

Revise 2 a) = 4, **b)** = 2, **c)** = 1, **d)** = 3

Revise 3 The following are true: a), b) and e).

Extend a) It is true because the text mentions a 'wedding anniversary'. **b)** It is true because the writer mentions the view of the North Sea in the first paragraph and later mentions not thinking about England. **c)** The writer refers to visiting their children 'in Australia and New Zealand' which implies one lives in Australia and the other in New Zealand. **d)** There is no indication whether it was or not. It was bought about 30 years ago but they could have owned another property before that. **e)** This is implied by 'we found that it was becoming harder to get insurance.' **f)** This is not implied. The fact that 'nobody mentioned erosion' might mean that nobody was aware of it or expected it.

Pages 10–11
Revise 1 a) enjoyed, **b)** neutral, **c)** did not enjoy, **d)** enjoyed, **e)** did not enjoy

Revise 2 a) that the writer is very fond of Roz / is very pleased to see her / is a demonstrative person; **b)** that the author has never seen Mark before or has not seen him for a long time; **c)** that Roz is the writer's sister and that she has children

Revise 3 a) The writer does not like the dinner lady; she is an 'ogress' and a 'jobsworth'; she is over zealous; she is like a prison guard; she carries out the orders of others; she is cruel. **b)** The writer thinks it is 'nonsense'; it is upsetting for children; it is oppressive; it is an example of government interference; it is ridiculous.

Extend The following are correct: a), c), f) and h).

Pages 12–13
Revise 1 The following are correct: b), c), f), i) and j).

Revise 2 a) One child ate six apples. **b)** I like apples and pears. **c)** Tommy fell from a tree. **d)** Do not leave this room.

Revise 3 The following are correct: b), f), h), i) and j).

Extend There are several ways of doing this. The following example has 59 words.

In the afternoon, the children played in the orchard. Their mother was in the house. Maisie said she was hungry so Tommy climbed a tree to get her an apple. John didn't think the tree was safe. Tommy ignored him. As he climbed along a bough, it cracked and broke. Tommy fell to the ground. He was in pain.

Pages 14–15
Revise 1

To express similarities	To express differences
similarly	on the other hand
both	however
also	but
in the same way	in contrast
	whereas

Revise 2 At least four from: the first took place in an orchard, the second in a back garden; Jake was watched by his parents, but Tommy wasn't; Jake was on a trampoline while Tommy was climbing a tree; Tommy was alone in the tree, whereas there were other children on the trampoline; Tommy fell accidentally but Jake was pushed; Tommy was hurt while Jake was not.

Revise 3

Source A	Source B
Dorothy went out straight after tea.	The writer played a game with the family after tea.
Dorothy seems to have spent the evening alone.	The writer was with other people.
The scenery during the walk was beautiful.	There was nothing to look at on the writer's walk.
Dorothy brought back one newspaper.	The writer brought back lots of newspapers, magazines and snacks.
The walk made Dorothy sad, although she cheered up later.	The walk to the village cheered up the writer, who stayed in a good mood.
Dorothy went to bed soon after getting home.	The writer stayed up late.

Extend Answers should be based on the differences identified in Revise 3. You should have written in complete sentences and used discourse markers/conjunctions to indicate contrast (e.g. 'whereas', 'but').

Pages 16–17
Revise 1 a) paraphrase, **b)** inverted commas, quotation marks (or the other way round), **c)** embedded, **d)** colon

Revise 2 a) = 4, **b)** = 2, **c)** = 3, **d)** = 1

Revise 3 a) 'pleasant cool but not cold'; **b)** 'spear-shaped streaks of polished steel'; **c)** 'melancholy' or 'saddest thoughts' or 'could not keep the tears within me'; **d)** 'felt it did me good'

Extend Answers might include: the change in mood brought about by the walk; her use of imagery to describe the scenery; the effect of the scenery on her; the use of adjectives such as 'melancholy' and 'solemn' to describe her mood and the implication that her experience of nature has partly caused these feelings; the 'confessional' aspect of the diary, expressing the writer's thoughts and emotions; the informal, almost note-like style.

Pages 18–19
Revise 1 a) Point, Evidence, Explanation (or Exploration) **b)** Point refers to making a new point about the text. Evidence means using a quote or a paraphrase to support your point. Explanation/exploration refers to analysing the quotation and exploring its connotations. **c)** No.

Revise 2 a) 'another idol has displaced'; **b)** 'They were a boy and a girl.'; **c)** 'tumultuous', 'uproarious'; **d)** 'The cold within him froze his old features.'; **e)** 'dark, empty house', 'lighted cheerfully'

Revise 3 a) Point: Romeo expresses his love by comparing Juliet to the sun, the moon and the stars: **Evidence:** 'It is the east and Juliet is the sun.' **Exploration:** This imagery demonstrates that his love is both great and natural. **b) Point:** By the end of the novel, Jane and Rochester's relationship has changed dramatically. **Evidence:** partly because he has been blinded in the fire. **Exploration:** It is almost as if she needs him to be dependent on her for the relationship to work. **c) Point:** Snowball, unlike Napoleon, **Evidence:** 'is full of plans for innovations and improvements'. **Exploration:** These three nouns all have positive connotations, connected with the future.

Extend Answers might include: the metaphor 'My mind ran' showing his excitement; the positive impression of her 'deep rich tones'; the 'strange mystery' suggesting that her being in danger is part of her attraction and she herself is a mystery; his speculation about her age and the connotations of it being 'sweet'; his attitude to being in love shown in the adjective 'dangerous'; his high regard for her; his feeling of unworthiness, indicated by 'weak' and 'weaker'; love seen as an adventure suggested by the verb 'dare'.

Pages 20–21
Revise 1 a) noun, **b)** verb, **c)** adjective, **d)** adverb, **e)** pronoun, **f)** preposition, **g)** conjunction, **h)** determiner

Revise 2 a) Sam, Ruby, **b)** action, courage, **c)** crew, **d)** building, flames, (fire) officers, equipment, house, children, **e)** they, he

Revise 3 a) determiner (the definite article), **b)** verb (in the simple past tense), **c)** (possessive) pronoun, **d)** conjunction, **e)** (abstract) noun, **f)** preposition, **g)** adverb, **h)** adjective

Extend Answers might include: the use of proper nouns such as 'Leatherhead' and 'London', which refer to real places, making the situation seem more real; the noun 'plan' showing he is in control; the active verb 'perceived' showing that he reacts coolly and plans carefully; the abstract nouns 'strength' and 'struggle' indicating the seriousness of what lies ahead; 'at once' and 'forthwith' showing the urgency of the situation; adverbs 'clearly' and 'inevitably' suggesting the seriousness of what will happen but in an understated manner; the general lack of adjectives contributing to the cool, rational tone of the piece, the exception being 'disastrous', its impact being increased because it is unusual.

Pages 22–23
Revise 1 a) = 2, b) = 1, c) = 4, d) = 3
Revise 2
1) a) formal, b) colloquial, c) dialectical, d) technical
2) a) 'could' or 'might', b) 'were offered' or 'had been baked', c) 'which'

Revise 3 a) 'was unfastened … loosed.'
b) The second sentence. c) 'The manager asked repeatedly did no one know …' d) 'A crowd which had followed him …' e) 'struggling to look through the glass panels.'

Extend Answers might include: the use of the passive voice making the man seem helpless and the actions impersonal; the active verbs in the compound sentence being neutral and unemotive, just saying what happened; the lack of answers to the manager's questions keeping the man's identity a mystery; the impression of the incident attracting attention, created comically by the idea of a 'crowd' following the 'immense' policeman and 'struggling' to see what was happening; the effect of the lack of any names.

Pages 24–25
Revise 1

	Type of imagery	Connotations
a)	pathetic fallacy (also personification)	The darkness of the clouds might reflect the mood of the narrator or another character. The rain is seen as the tears being wept by the cloud, whose darkness is associated with anger (as in 'a black mood').
b)	metaphor	She is likely to 'erupt' at any minute and cause damage, like an unstoppable natural force.
c)	simile	He is terrified and vulnerable, like a small animal in danger.
d)	personification	Love is like a person or perhaps an army that cannot be resisted.

Revise 2

Technique	Example	Effect
Onomatopoeia	clanged	The sound conveys the suddenness of the loud noise.
Alliteration	dark, dank, dirty	The harsh sounds convey the unpleasantness of the experience.
Assonance	'Go slowly over to the open window.'	The succession of long 'o's slows down the speech, reflecting the calm instruction.
Sibilance (also alliteration)	Speaking softly, Sophie	The 's' sounds convey the gentle tone of voice.

Revise 3 a) war b) She sees life as difficult/full of problems to be overcome. c) She felt she was in a safe place but it is no longer the case and to keep safe she needs to move. d) 'another pitched battle must be fought with fortune' suggests that fate or luck always seems to work against her but she is prepared to keep fighting (showing a belief in free will and her own strength of mind). e) 'But what road was open – what plan available?' suggests that at the moment she does not know what to do but she is going to think through her problems and come up with an answer.

Extend Answers should be based on the responses above and should include: the connotations of seeing life as a war and what it tells us about her character; her feeling that life is against her; her determination and strength of character reflected in the development of the metaphor; her thoughtfulness shown in her consideration of what to do next.

Pages 26–27
Revise 1 a) repetition, b) hyperbole, c) triplet, d) emotive language, e) rhetorical question

Revise 2 There are many possible answers, for example: a) As **frail, nervous** Bertie walked **gingerly** down the street, he was approached by a **huge, terrifying** stranger. **Menacingly,** the man **demanded** money from Bertie. A **frightened** Bertie refused to give him anything. b) As **rich, arrogant** Bertie walked **confidently** down the street, he was approached by a **nervous, bedraggled** stranger. **Politely,** the man **begged for** money from Bertie. A **selfish** Bertie refused to give him anything.

Revise 3 a) 'What action did they take?', 'Why on earth would she ring the police?', 'So that they could give her another leaflet?' b) 'frail', 'terrifying ordeal', 'vulnerable', 'courage', 'ruthless' c) 'locking her doors at night, installing a burglar alarm and ringing the police' d) 'beyond words'

Extend Answers might include: the use of emotive language and hyperbole to create sympathy for the victim; the use of repetition to emphasise certain points; rhetorical questions used, expecting a certain answer; the sense of outrage created by the contrast between the 'terrifying ordeal' and the police's 'leaflets'.

Pages 28–29
Revise 1 a) = 2, b) = 4, c) = 1, d) = 3

Revise 2 Possible answers include: a) This novel ends with a character's death, bringing the story to a neat conclusion, but possibly leaving the reader feeling sad. b) The writer leaves the reader with a feeling of being included in a happy ending. The writer reaches out to the reader. c) This novel ends with a happy ending for the main characters, leaving the reader satisfied with the outcome. d) This ending is ambiguous. The character disappears, ending the story, but there is a possibility that he could survive and return.

Revise 3 a) He is married/he has a regular routine. b) She fusses over him/she is a creature of habit/she does not really understand him. c) He feels that they are stuck in a routine/he does not seem to feel any love or affection for his wife. d) 'precisely our usual manner', 'the level kiss of domesticity', 'no fear of the extemporaneous', 'no fear of … variety spicing her infinite custom' e) 'I had no cold', 'her infinite custom', 'long malpractice', 'dabbed awry my well-set scarf pin' f) Answers might include: he does not return after work; he plots to murder her; he gets involved with another woman; we find out that she has a secret life.

Extend Answers might include: the use of the first-person narrator; it starts as an ordinary day but the use of 'seemed' implies it will turn out not to be; the inclusion of small details of married life; the sense conveyed of the narrator's mood; the distance between the couple; the way that readers might empathise with one of the characters.

Pages 30–31
Revise 1 The correct order is: b), a), d), c), e).

Revise 2 a) Part of the story that happened before the main narrative begins and is referred back to. b) Starting with a general overview and gradually focusing in on smaller details. c) Referring back to the beginning of a text at the end. d) Starting with the last event and going backwards.

Revise 3 a) 'The next evening' b) It sets the scene. c) He moves from a description of the general scene as it is at any time to a particular time and a description of the gig. d) From describing the gig, he moves closer to describe the people in it, starting with the man before changing focus to the woman.

Extend Answers might include: the use of 'big to small' in the description; shift of focus from the gig to the man and then to the woman; the sense that they are being observed; Hardy keeping their identities from the reader; the contrast between them; the way they are placed in the landscape; the sense of their position and class; what the reader might infer from the descriptions of the characters.

Pages 32–33
Revise 1 The following are true: a), c), d), f), g), h) and i)

Revise 2 a) = 2, b) = 7, c) = 5, d) = 6, e) = 3, f) = 1, g) = 4

Revise 3
a) He was a butcher
b) Determined
c) Have affairs with other women
d) She goes and sleeps in a neighbour's house

Extend The protagonist is Mrs Mooney as she is introduced to the reader and described in detail. The antagonist is Mr Mooney – he makes life difficult for his wife. The inciting incident is when he attacks her with the meat cleaver, as from now on her life will be different.

Pages 34–35
Revise 1 a) = 7, **b)** = 1, **c)** = 6, **d)** = 3, **e)** = 2, **f)** = 5, **g)** = 4
Revise 2 a) omniscient narrator; **b)** (reliable) first-person narrator; **c)** intrusive narrator

Revise 3 a) omniscient narrator; **b)** 'shabby', 'stooped' or 'little' – they give an impression of someone who is unimportant, unimpressive, weak, poor; **c)** 'cunningly', 'firmly' – they give the impression that she is clever, in control, professionally successful; **d)** Repetition of 'white' adds to the impression of Mr Mooney being old and weak.

Extend Answers might include: the straightforward, unemotional giving of facts; the portrayal of Mr Mooney as old and weak; the contrast with the strength of Mrs Mooney; Mrs Mooney introduced as an active force; adjectives and adverbs used to describe her emphasising her strength of character; the shift of focus to her boarding house; the sense given of its varied inhabitants; the connotations of Mrs Mooney's nickname.

Pages 36–37
Revise 1 The following are correct: a), c), e) and f).

Revise 2

Quotation	How we learn about Silas Marner	What we learn about Silas Marner
Again he put his trembling hands to his head, and gave a wild ringing scream, the cry of desolation.	d	He is extremely upset and emotional.
He was believed to be a young man of exemplary life and ardent faith.	e	He is well thought of by others and is both religious and virtuous.
He was then simply a pallid young man, with prominent, short-sighted brown eyes.	a	He is pale and short-sighted with big eyes.
'Robbed!' said Silas gaspingly. 'I've been robbed! I want the constable and the Justice – and Squire Cass – and Mr Crackenthorp.'	b	He is angry and excited because he has been robbed. He might be a bit confused but is determined to get justice.
'And he's took care of me and loved me from the first, and I'll cleave to him as long as he lives, and nobody shall ever come between him and me.' (Eppie)	c	The speaker loves and respects Silas. They are extremely close.

Revise 3 Answers might include: **a)** She is 'tall, thin and brown' and 'reminded one of a young colt'. **b)** She has a strong 'decided' character but is also 'funny' and 'thoughtful'. She can be changeable.
Extend Answers should develop the responses to Revise 3 and include comment on the use of physical description to give insight into character; the writer's listing of Jo's physical and mental characteristics; and the comparison of her to a colt.

Pages 38–39
Revise 1 The following are true: b), c), d) and e).
Revise 2 a) = 3, **b)** = 2, **c)** = 5, **d)** = 1, **e)** = 4
Revise 3 Answers might include **a)** He is a drinker/he is a 'hard case'/he is sociable/he swears/he can be aggressive. **b)** She is 'lively'/flirtatious/pretty/likes to sing. **c)** She does not seem to have control over Jack. She keeps an eye on Polly and keeps her away from her father, so she is protective to a certain extent, but she encourages both of her children to socialise with the lodgers. She might be thinking of finding a husband for Polly among the lodgers.
Extend Building on the responses to Revise 3, answers might include: the contrast between the attitude to son and daughter; implied traditional gender roles; the vivid picture of life in the boarding house and the freedom given to her children to join in; the importance of entertainment in their lives; use of colloquial language such as 'hard case'; imagery used to describe Polly ('perverse madonna'); Mrs Mooney's constant presence and the sense that she is in control; the ambiguity of her attitude to Polly.

Pages 40–41
Revise 1 The following are true: a), c), e), f), h) and i).
Revise 2 a) Any three from: biography, autobiography, travel writing, magazine/newspaper articles, reviews, diaries, letters. **b)** Any three from: inform, explain, argue, persuade, entertain, describe, advise. **c)** Viewpoints and perspectives are the writers' opinions, ideas and feelings about the subject they are writing about.
Revise 3 The following are true: a), d), e) and g).
Extend Answers might include: use of generally positive diction; a variety of reasons given for visiting, appealing to different groups; contrasting adjectives such as 'dramatic' and 'tranquil'; hyperbole such as 'countless'; list of three; alliteration.

Page 42–43
Revise 1 a) = 5, **b)** = 2, **c)** = 3, **d)** = 4, **e)** = 1
Revise 2 a) opinion pieces, **b)** views, **c)** anecdote, **d)** cliched **e)** imagery **f)** journalists **g)** heartfelt, **h)** perspective, **i)** rhetorical, **j)** hyperbolic
Revise 3 a) He says 'I think'. **b)** 'stamped'. The verb is violent and expresses the sense that something has been forced on him that he cannot remove easily. **c)** Three from 'rottenest', 'rottenness', 'deformed', 'frowsy'. They give the impression of something that has gone wrong and become unpleasant to the senses. **d)** The repetition of 'sometimes' gives an impression of how common this is but also how examples vary. It gives the feeling of being surrounded by these unattractive things.
Extend Answers should build on the answers to Revise 3, using quotations, developing points in more detail and connecting the points using discourse markers.

Pages 44–45
Revise 1 The following are correct: a), b), e) and f).
Revise 2 a) = 2, **b)** = 4, **c)** = 1, **d)** = 3
Revise 3

Source A	Source B
Set in France (abroad)	Set in Dorset
Luxury/facilities including pool	'rough and ready' with basic facilities
'waited on' by servants/adults	Had to 'muck in' doing chores
No other children	Lots of children
'bored'	'never bored'

Extend Answers should focus on and develop the points made in the answer to Revise 3.

Pages 46–47
Revise 1 The following are true: a), c), d), e), f) and g).
Revise 2 a) A – 'Don't miss it!' **b)** A – 'like a hungry wolf' **c)** B – 'draw a veil' **d)** B – e.g. 'I really have to …'

Revise 3

	Text A (Lake Garda travel guide)	Text B (*Pictures from Italy*)
What is the writer's attitude to the place?	He/she praises its beauty and attractions.	He finds it unpleasant and ugly.
What is the purpose of the text?	To persuade people to visit the area.	To give an informative and entertaining account of the writer's travels.
How would you describe the general tone of the piece?	Positive, upbeat, enthusiastic, uncritical	Negative, descriptive, critical
Comment on the writer's use of sentence structures.	Four long sentences, two of them complex, allowing the writer to give explanations and develop descriptions using subordinate clauses.	Long sentences, using lists, broken up by semi-colons to give a detailed description.
Comment on the writer's use of language features	Uses common images to create a sense of beauty; positive diction to persuade readers; alliteration to make it seem relaxing; cliched images when describing scenery.	Use of negative diction to build up an unpleasant picture; anaphora of 'something' used to build a sense of oppression; alliteration (and oxymoron) of 'frowsy fragrance' to amuse reader.

Extend Answers should focus on and develop ideas from Revise 3, explaining the writers' attitudes and methods in greater detail and referring directly to the text.

Pages 48–59

Exam Practice, Paper 1 For questions 2 to 4 of each practice paper, use the mark scheme below to self-assess your strengths and weaknesses. Work up from the bottom, putting a tick by things you have fully accomplished, a ½ by skills that are in place but need securing, and underlining areas that need particular development. The estimated grade boundaries are included so you can assess your progress towards your target grade.

Question 2

Grade	AO2
7+ (7–8 marks)	You have: • analysed the effects of the writer's choice of language • used an appropriate range of quotations • used sophisticated subject terminology appropriately.
5–6 (5–6 marks)	You have: • clearly explained the effects of the writer's choice of language • used an appropriate range of quotations • used subject terminology appropriately.
3–4 (3–4 marks)	You have: • attempted to comment on the effects of the writer's choice of language • used some appropriate textual references • used some subject terminology, usually appropriately.
1–2 (1–2 marks)	You have: • made some simple comment on the effects of the writer's choice of language • used some simple references to the text • made simple use of subject terminology, not always appropriately.

Question 3

Grade	AO2
7+ (7–8 marks)	You have: • analysed the effects of the writer's choice of structural features • used a range of appropriate examples • used sophisticated subject terminology appropriately.
5–6 (5–6 marks)	You have: • clearly explained the effects of the writer's choice of structural features • used a range of relevant examples • used subject terminology appropriately.
3–4 (3–4 marks)	You have: • attempted to comment on the effects of the writer's choice of structural features • used some appropriate examples • used some subject terminology, usually appropriately.
1–2 (1–2 marks)	You have: • made some simple comment on the effects of structural features • used some simple examples • made simple use of subject terminology, not always appropriately.

Question 4

Grade	AO4
7+ (16–20 marks)	You have: • evaluated critically and in detail the effect on the reader • shown perceptive understanding of the writer's methods • selected a range of appropriate textual detail • developed a convincing critical response to the focus of the statement.
5–6 (11–15 marks)	You have: • evaluated clearly the effect on the reader • shown clear understanding of the writer's methods • selected a range of relevant textual detail • made a clear and relevant response to the focus of the statement.
3–4 (6–10 marks)	You have: • made some evaluative comments on the effect on the reader • shown some understanding of the writer's methods • selected some appropriate textual detail • made some response to the focus of the statement.
1–2 (1–5 marks)	You have: • made simple comments on the effect on the reader • shown limited understanding of the writer's methods • selected some simple textual detail • made a simple, limited response to the focus of the statement.

Below are some of the ideas that might be included in your responses. However, bear in mind that the content of the best answers will be very varied and sometimes highly original.

Pages 48–50

Question 1
a) Small
b) Seven full waggons
c) A cantering colt is faster
d) A hedge

Question 2 Answers might include: the sense of power and size created by words such as 'thumped', 'heavily' and 'slow' contrasted with the woman who is 'insignificantly trapped'; how this gives a sense of opposition between human and machine; references to nature creating a sense of gloom and lack of life caused by both the time and season ('withered oak leaves' and 'dusk') and by industry ('forsaken', 'abandoned', 'stagnant'); personification of dusk; power of industry expressed in the heavy sound of the active verb 'loomed'; simile and personification in 'flames like red sores licking' creating an unpleasant image; contrast between 'clumsy' and 'spinning fast' in the description of the colliery; long sentence used to describe 'inevitable' movement of the train; use of lists to build up description; change from complex to compound sentences when the colliery is described; the effect of the very short simple sentence (and passive voice) at the end.

Question 3 Answers might include: opening focused on the train; the use of the train to introduce contrast between industry and humanity; use of the train to bring the reader into the town; contrast in the opening paragraph between industry and nature; use of a short, one-sentence paragraph, contrasting with the long opening paragraph, to change focus from train to colliery; third paragraph opens with a reference to the men before changing focus to the house and introducing the woman; continuation of the industry versus nature theme with the description of the garden; next paragraph moves to description of the woman; the boy hiding in the bushes; the mention of the brook; the return to the train, now identified as being driven by the boy's grandfather.

Question 4 Answers might include: the way the woman is not initially named; the way in which she is placed in her environment; the possible significance of the focus on the garden in contrast with the mining town; the language used to describe nature in the garden ('ragged', 'dishevelled', etc.) perhaps reflecting the woman's struggles in life (pathetic fallacy); physical description suggesting a strong personality ('imperious', 'definite') and a kind of nobility that might seem out of place in her environment; juxtaposition of 'calm' and 'disillusionment' intriguing readers and making them wonder how she became like that; description of the boy suggesting he is a similar character ('sturdy', 'defiantly'); the way in which she moves from harshness ('sternly') to being conciliating and speaking 'gently'; the extent to which this might be typical of a mother; the presence of her son and reference to his grandfather suggesting that she is at the centre of an extended family.

Pages 51–53

Question 1
a) It is rather better
b) It is vigorous, shapely and healthy
c) The King's Head pub
d) Anything over £80

Question 2 Answers might include: the omniscient narrator giving the account from Tom's point of view; sense of Tom's pride in showing off his bull shown by its 'solitary state'; use of mixed metaphor to describe and humanise the bull; 'grass widower of a grazing harem' paradoxically suggesting both power and lack of power; focus on Tom's attitude to his brother expressed in the use of the adjectives 'languid' and 'patronising'; the two examples which show the differences between the brothers by juxtaposing contrasting sights which appeal to one or the other ('potato crop'/'yellow flowering weed' and 'black-faced lambs'/'foliage'); positive, hyperbolic language used to show Tom's feelings about the bull ('crowning pride and glory', 'many excellences … redoubtable'); the long complex sentences used to reflect the rambling nature of the walk and the complexity of Tom's reactions.

Question 3 Answers might include: how the extract starts by focusing on the bull and its importance to Tom; the importance of the bull in commercial terms and Tom's pride in it; long second paragraph focusing on Tom and Laurence's relationship through a description of their walk to see the bull; the second part of the paragraph referring in flashback to Tom's earlier visit to Taunton and Laurence's painting; the end of the paragraph returning to the farm and the real bull; focus on the bull as Tom takes Laurence into the yard; use of direct speech and indirect speech to convey Laurence's attitude to the bull and move focus to Laurence's painting; the impact of the final statement of the conversation; the final short paragraph returning to the theme of the bull's market value and to Tom's feelings.

Question 4 Answers might include: the way in which the story is told in the third person but from Tom's point of view; the way in which readers are already aware of Tom's pride in the bull and his antipathy towards Laurence and Laurence's way of life; the language used to diminish Laurence's achievement ('good of its kind') and his pride in it ('inordinately pleased'); the emphasis on Tom's bull being 'real' and the feeling that his achievement in breeding a real bull is superior; a possible reaction from readers that Tom's dislike of Laurence makes him dismissive of his achievement; Tom's assumption that his work is more valuable, perhaps not shared by everyone; a sense that Tom and Laurence may be as bad as each other in 'showing off' their respective bulls; Tom's rudeness about Laurence's picture of a bull 'standing in some slush'; Laurence's unattractive 'complacency'; a sense that Tom's attitude causes him to show off about the money he has made; sympathy for Tom feeling that his hard work is unappreciated and not well-rewarded.

Pages 54–56

Question 1
a) They are so keen to get to school
b) She is the eldest
c) They say nothing
d) She is bossy

Question 2 Answers might include: direct speech used to express Isabel's dominance; passive voice expressing mother's authority ('it had been arranged'); use of ellipsis at the end of the second paragraph giving a sense of the girls' anticipation; verbs 'jangle' and 'whip' to indicate the activity of arriving at school; third-person narrator conveying the girls' feelings; impact of short sentences; list of the girls' responses to Isabel building up a sense of their attitude to her, using words such as 'flatteringly' and 'special'; the metaphorical 'held quite a court' showing her importance by comparing her to a queen.

Question 3 Answers might include: the extract starting with the girls' excitement over the doll's house; how the beginning focuses on their reaction to it and the importance of showing off; the establishment of Isabel as the boss; the explanation of the plan and what might happen later; the focus moving with the girls into the playground and their relationships with the other children; the end of the seventh paragraph introducing the Kelveys and their exclusion from the group; focus then shifting to the differences between the families at the school, how they all came to be at the same school and how social differences are reflected at school; the next paragraph moving from other people's reactions to a more detailed description of the Kelveys and their circumstances; the last paragraph returning the reader to Isabel talking about the doll's house.

Question 4 Answers might include: the way society is reflected in the school; the variety of backgrounds of those who go to the school; the way the writer gives an overview of small-town life; the hierarchy in the school; the contrast between the Burnells at one end of the social scale and the Kelveys at the other; the way the Kelveys are physically shunned; the teacher's attitude to them; the sympathy gained for them by the description of their mother; awareness that the way their mother dresses them does not help them to fit in; the fact that the parents have forbidden the other children to speak to the Kelveys; possible sense that the children are not being actively cruel but just reflecting their parents' attitudes; the way our Else is depicted as a vulnerable victim; the competitive nature of relationships in school; Isabel as the dominant child, using her position and her power; whether the children's attitudes are cruel or just normal.

Pages 57–59

Question 1
a) On a stile
b) Indigestion
c) He blames the world
d) To try to enjoy the spring

Question 2 Answers might include: use of the past perfect or pluperfect tense ('he had') to indicate that it is a kind of flashback; colloquial language used in direct speech to show informality and the class of the speakers; contrast of this with the formal tone of the narrative, using words such as 'sinister' (to mean left) to give it a humorous tone; words such as 'trembling', 'wrathful' and 'fury' to show the strength of his reaction to a trivial matter; the absurdity of the situation with the cap; comic tone created by repetition of 'askew'; the ellipsis showing his inability to find an appropriate word; the use of short sentences to describe his actions.

Question 3 Answers might include: unusual use of direct speech to introduce the protagonist and his mood; comic effect of his talking to himself in the first paragraph; focus on him at the beginning and remaining on him throughout; time change between the second and third paragraph to a flashback to earlier in the day; introduction of his wife through her speech and action; short paragraphs and direct speech conveying Mr Polly's mood and actions; his exit leading to the focus shifting to Mrs Polly and through her to a description of their meal, going further back into the past (a sort of reverse chronological order developing); long paragraph detailing the food focusing on the couple's everyday existence; focus returns at the end of the extract to Mr Polly; how the final section returns the reader to the time and place where the extract starts, as Mr Polly asks himself a question which the reader might expect will lead to the story of his earlier life.

Question 4 Answers might include: the reader's awareness of Mr Polly's unhappiness from the first part of the extract; the comic effect of his childish slang; the exaggerated response to the trivial problem of the cap; the use of this episode to express his general dissatisfaction; direct speech exclamation used to express his unhappiness and anger; comedy from the violence shown to the cap; the establishment of the Pollys' 'ordinariness' by the way their lower middle-class lifestyle is described; Mrs Polly reacting as if he were a child ('tantrums'); the detailed description of their meal, especially the list of pickles; the repetition of 'hated' showing the strength of his feelings; readers' potential reactions to his apparently sudden change in mood from lunch, which he ate 'with every appearance of appetite, and indeed with avidity'; the intrusive narrator's comment 'there seems to be no pleasing some people.'

Exam Practice, Paper 2

Pages 60–72

For questions 2–4 of each practice paper, use the mark scheme below to self-assess your strengths and weaknesses. Work up from the bottom, putting a tick by things you have fully accomplished, a ½ by skills that are in place but need securing, and underlining areas that need particular development. The estimated grade boundaries are included so you can assess your progress towards your target grade.

Question 2

Grade	AO1
7+ (7–8 marks)	You have: • given a perceptive interpretation of both texts • synthesised evidence from the texts • used appropriate quotations from both texts.
5–6 (5–6 marks)	You have: • started to interpret both texts • shown clear connections between the texts • used relevant quotations from both texts.
3–4 (3–4 marks)	You have: • tried to infer from one or both texts • tried to link evidence from the texts • used some quotations from one or both texts.
1–2 (1–2 marks)	You have: • paraphrased text • made simple or no links between the texts • referred to one or both texts.

Question 3

Grade	AO2
7+ (10–12 marks)	You have: • analysed the effects of the writer's choice of language • used a range of appropriate quotations • used sophisticated subject terminology appropriately.
5–6 (7–9 marks)	You have: • clearly explained the effects of the writer's choice of language • used a range of relevant quotations • used subject terminology appropriately.
3–4 (4–6 marks)	You have: • commented on the effects of the writer's choice of language • used some relevant quotations • used some subject terminology, not always appropriately.
1–2 (1–3 marks)	You have: • tried to comment on the effects of the writer's choice of language • referred to the text • mentioned subject terminology.

Question 4

Grade	AO3
7+ (13–16 marks)	You have: • compared ideas and perspectives in a perceptive way • analysed methods used to convey ideas and perspectives • used a range of appropriate quotations from both texts.
5–6 (9–12 marks)	You have: • compared ideas and perspectives in a clear and relevant way • explained clearly methods used to convey ideas and perspectives • used relevant quotations from both texts.
3–4 (5–8 marks)	You have: • identified some differences between ideas and perspectives • commented on methods used to convey ideas and perspectives • used some quotations from one or both texts.
1–2 (1–4 marks)	You have: • referred to different ideas and perspectives • identified how differences are conveyed • made simple references to one or both texts.

Below are some of the ideas that might be included in your responses. However, bear in mind that the content of the best answers will be very varied and sometimes highly original.

Pages 60–62

Question 1 The correct answers are a), d), e) and h).

Question 2 Answers might include: Tabby and Miss Branwell looked after the Brontës at the same time in different ways, whereas Ripley had one carer at a time; Tabby stayed for a long time but Ripley's carers came and went frequently; Tabby and Miss Branwell lived with the Brontës, Mrs Snedwell and her replacement did not live with the Ripleys but we are not told whether others did or not; Miss Branwell was a relative of the family but Ripley had no relatives to call on; the Brontës were educated at home but Lottie Ripley was taken to and picked up from school; the Brontës' carers were generally more mature and reliable than the Ripleys' (with the exception of Mrs Snedwell).

Question 3 Answers might include: use of past perfect tense to describe events in the distant past (before the main action being described); references to particular places setting the scene; suggestion of Tabby's age through reference to 'pack horses', etc. and contrast with the time of writing ('that was when …'); use of dialect words 'beck' and 'bottom' to describe the landscape reflecting Tabby's own speech; Tabby's direct speech showing her origins; her belief in the fairies conveyed without comment as a fact ('had known folk') and the sense of something magical transferred to her; the long list of things she 'no doubt' told 'tales' about conveying both her gossipy nature and her influence on the children and their writing.

Question 4 Answers might include: Source A being first person and Source B third person; Gaskell being more distant from the issues which concern another family in the past, whereas Ripley is writing about issues that affect her now; Gaskell's warm description of Tabby reflecting the attitudes of the children to her, which is to some extent mirrored in Ripley's description of Mrs Snedwell but not of the other carers; similarities between Tabby and Mrs Snedwell; Source A's assumption that readers might have similar problems and would sympathise; her focus on how it makes life hard for her contrasting with Source B's focus on the character of Tabby and how she helped the children; the extent to which the two situations reflect practice and expectations of the times when they were written; the lack of any criticism of Tabby's and Miss Branwell's care contrasting with Ripley's attitude to all except Mrs Snedwell; the way in which Miss Branwell is a family member and Tabby is treated as a family member whereas Ripley resents having to get involved with the emotional problems of the carers; the different purposes of the pieces, Ripley aiming to entertain and put forward her opinion of childcare issues while Gaskell's purpose is to give an insight into how her subject (Charlotte Brontë) was brought up and became a writer.

Pages 63–65

Question 1 The correct answers are b), c), e) and g).

Question 2 Answers might include: the Ragged School has been set up by a religious group but Phoebe's is a 'state school'; the Ragged School takes all ages whereas the schools Stringer describes are primary schools; the Ragged School teachers have little influence on the pupils but the modern headteachers are bureaucratic and interfere in the children's lives; the Ragged School boys are described as 'cunning' and 'wicked' and

many of the girls are 'wretched', while the pupils at Phoebe's school are 'bright' and 'happy'; the Ragged School is 'foul' whereas Phoebe's school is 'lovely'.

Question 3 Answers might include: the use of a rhetorical question to interest the reader in the subject; the conscious use of the repeated cliché 'health and safety gone mad'; the use of exclamation marks to express strength of emotion; the use of the first-person plural ('we') to involve the readers and get them to empathise; the conversational, colloquial tone; the comical hyperbole of 'ogress' with connotations of fairy tales; the use of repetition/parallel phrasing to describe the chain of command; the impact of the short sentence at the end of the second paragraph; the 'apology' at the start of the fourth paragraph and the use of 'we' and 'our' to assert the importance of the parents; the connotations of the hyperbole 'Health Fascists', with the potential to both amuse and offend.

Question 4 Answers might include: a contrast between the extreme seriousness of Dickens' concerns and what some might consider the triviality of Stringer's; Dickens' sense that the state is doing too little opposed to Stringer's assertion that it is doing too much; Stringer's focus on parents contrasting with the lack of any reference to parents in Source A; concerns of both writers with literacy but the high figures quoted by Stringer not coming close to the problem in Dickens' day; Dickens is concerned about basic education whereas Stringer is concerned about the system interfering in matters that he does not think of as its responsibility; Stringer's mixture of outrage and a desire to entertain compared with Dickens' desire to shock by describing what he has seen; Dickens' use of emotive language in describing the school and Stringer's use of comic hyperbole; Dickens' letter being about the children of the poor whereas Stringer focuses on his own child; Dickens' letter seen as part of a campaign; Dickens' focus on persuading his readers of a need for basic education while Stringer assumes that is provided.

Pages 66–68

Question 1 The correct answers are c), d), g) and h).

Question 2 Answers might include: the post offices in Source B are very busy but those in Source A are losing customers; in Source A the sub-postmaster gets a salary of £12,000 a year, while the Source B sub-postmasters get 12s6d per week; the offices in Source B deal in 'telegraph messages' and 'money-orders' whereas the main business in Westerley is parcels and people drawing out money; village post offices in Source B serve a population of about 1000 but in Westerley it is 10,000; the opening hours in Source B are longer, from seven until eight or later (including weekends) whereas Westerley post office is open from nine until five-thirty on weekdays.

Question 3 Answers might include: formality of language including vocabulary ('emoluments') and use of the passive voice ('was … highly esteemed'); irony of statements about postmasters' criminal behaviour, which the writer clearly does not believe; the use of the third-person singular ('he') to present a typical sub-postmaster, implying the problems are general; insulting language in 'some village somebody' and the slang metaphor 'bigwig' to criticise those in authority; use of the present tense; repetition of 'he gets'; comparison with poets emphasising the skill and hard work involved in the job of postmaster and implying that writing poetry is easy in comparison and perhaps that poets are lazy; the use of the quotation 'a man and a brother' to appeal to religious feelings/empathy.

Question 4 Answers might include: differing perspectives, the first from the point of view of a villager but including the postmaster's views while the second, though claiming to not be from a sub-postmaster, clearly looks at things from a sub-postmaster's perspective; Source A sees the post office as a community asset, while Source B sees it as a practical business, though still stressing its importance to the community; both writers feel that sub-postmasters are underpaid and their work undervalued; both mention other sources of income being needed; Source A refers to the decline in post office business whereas Source B is about how busy it is; Source A is about a local issue which could have a more general application, Source B is making a point which applies to the whole country and does not give specific examples; Source B talks about 'the sub-postmaster', customers and supervisors in general terms while Source A uses names ('Alice', 'Sid and Else') to personalise the issue; Source B is more overtly political than Source A, mentioning a statement in parliament, but Source A refers to decisions made by the Post Office which affect local services; Source A has a chatty, colloquial tone while Source B is more formal; Source A appeals to the villagers to save the post office while Source B appeals to the 'public' to respond to the postmasters' complaints.

Pages 69–72

Question 1 The correct answers are a), b), e) and g).

Question 2 Answers might include: the Source A party is for adults ('ladies and gentlemen') and Source B for children/teenagers; the Source A event is in the host and hostess's house while the Source B event could be in a school or hotel; Source A involves alcohol but Source B does not; Source A mentions a lot of rules on how to behave but rules are not specified in Source B except for what the guests are not allowed to bring; Source A guests are collected by carriages while Source B mentions a lot of different possible modes of transport; Source A guests have the hosts' servants to help them while Source B guests have school staff and venue staff; Source B is to celebrate a special occasion but Source A does not mention a specific reason for the party.

Question 3 Answers might include: quotation of cliched sayings; use of capitals to humorously stress teenagers' priorities; lists of items to convey expense involved; use of the second person to address readers directly, assuming their interest in the subject; chatty tone; use of modal verbs and conditionals ('if') to give advice politely, expressing possibilities; some irony ('blessed with'); bracketed aside giving a sense of sharing a joke; direct address using imperative ('forget').

Question 4 Answers might include: both texts aim to give advice to their readers; Source A is aimed at well-off middle-class Victorians, whereas Source B is aimed at modern parents; Source A is aimed at the hostess and Source B at the guest's parents; Source B focuses a lot on cost, which is not mentioned in Source A; Source A is concerned about the proper behaviour of hosts and guests at the party while Source B is more about preparation and tells readers not to worry about the party itself; Source A has a fairly formal tone, using the passive voice and third person, whereas Source B addresses readers directly in a chatty tone; both sources, nevertheless, seek to reassure their readers and make them feel less anxious about the parties; both sources break up the text, the first using headings in capitals integrated into new paragraphs, the second using subheadings; Source A conveys established conventions as rules to be followed ('should') whereas Source B questions the conventions.